Church Organization

~

What Do I Do?

A Quick Guide to Organizing Your Church

By

Janie Sheeley-Torain, EdD

Church Organization

~

What Do I Do?

A Quick Guide to Organizing Your Church

By

Janie Sheeley-Torain, EdD

Copyright

Acknowledgement

To God who is the center of my life! God gets the honor and glory for providing me with spiritual leaders and a companion after God's own heart.

To my husband, Deacon Nathaniel, for his persistent support, input and encouragement. Thank you for the compliments and the constructive criticism.

To my children, grandchildren, and great grandchildren inspiring me to keep a close relationship with God.

And to my pastor, deacons, deaconesses, the fivefold ministry, and the many fine disciples of God with whom I have had the honor to serve with.

Appreciation is expressed and credit is given to the following for the information included:

Church Staff Administration, Practical Approaches, by Leonard e. Wedel (copyright 1978)

Personnel Administration Guide for Southern Baptist Churches, compiled by Tim J. Holcomb (copyright 1988)

"Broadmoor Baptist Church Personnel Manual May 1990" (Broadmoor Baptist Church, Madison, Mississippi)

"Keeping Your Church out of Court" (Legal issues notebook), available from the pastor/Leadership

development department, Mississippi Baptist
Convention Board

Contents

This publication is produced to aid a church in organizing its staff and in writing job descriptions for the staff members, committees and officers. It is intended to serve only as a guide, with each church developing its unique organization.

Scriptures referenced are taken from the Blue Letter Bible King James Version online at https://www.blueletterbible.org/ unless otherwise noted in the other sources referenced in the footnotes.

Given the transient nature of online publications, it is possible a web address may no longer be active or may have been altered since the print date of this book.

Introduction

Congratulations! You have taken a step of faith toward what is a desire in your heart. You are to be commended for acquiring resources, for example this book, to assist in your endeavors. Before going any further, let's establish a few terms that you will see throughout this book. The word "church' has come to be known as the public building in which we attend to worship so that is how we will use the word "church" in this book. However, 'The Church" is the organization of baptized believers such and the whole body of Christians. Keeping this in mind, I would like to discuss "The Church" first before going on to discuss the church building.

Whether you have a store front or a stadium, the structure of your church determines how fast you will grow and the size to which you will grow (Warren, 2016[i]) Since we are referring to organizing for effectiveness, any structure, no matter what, should be organized with a purpose and around the gifts of the people within it. First God wants us to organize around the purposes for which he created the Church. Acts 2:42 could be considered a purpose statement for the church:

"They devoted themselves to the apostles' teaching and to the fellowship, to the breaking of bread and to prayer."

According to this verse, the purposes or activities of the church should be:

- ◆ Teaching biblical doctrine
- ◆ Providing a place of fellowship for believers
- ◆ Observing the Lord's supper
- ◆ Praying
- ◆ Going about doing good

Another commission given to the church is proclaiming the gospel of salvation through Jesus Christ. The church is called to be faithful in sharing the gospel through word and deed. The church is to be a "light" in the community, pointing people toward our Lord and Savior Jesus Christ. The Church is to both promote the gospel and prepare its members to proclaim the gospel. Some other purposes of the church are given in James 1:27 "...To visit the fatherless and widows in their affliction, and to keep himself unspotted from the world." (KJV)

Paul gave an excellent illustration to the believers in Corinth as to the purpose of the church when he said the church is God's hands, mouth, and feet in this world—the body of Christ (I Corinthians 12:12-27 KJV). We are to be doing the things that Jesus Christ would do if He were here physically on the earth. The church is to be "Christian," "Christ-like", and Christ-following.

Second, God wants us to organize around the talents and gifts of our membership—spiritual and vocational. God gave spiritual gifts for the perfecting of the saints, for the work of the ministry, and for the edifying of the body of Christ (Ephesians 4:12 KJV). You will find more detailed information in Chapter 1 Look for the Spiritual Gifts.

Our vocational skills are empirical skills that individuals acquire in a specific area of interest. Vocational skills are more practical and deal with our jobs and careers—but are still God given. Deuteronomy 8:18 states

"But thou shalt remember the Lord thy God; for it is he that giveth thee power to get wealth that he may establish his covenant which he sware unto thy fathers, as it is this day." (KJV)

God gives each of his children one motivational gift at salvation, and he bestows the ministry gifts and manifestation gifts as he pleases. God strategically places the members of the Body of Christ-with their variety of God-given gifts and vocational skills in the Body. Ideally, these members do not function independently as servants of God; rather they function as a healthy contributing member of the Church.

Knowing that each of us has gifts and vocational skills that are valuable and needed in the Body of Christ gives us purpose in God's kingdom. As we demonstrate the love of God through gifts that he gives us, we can experience personal fulfillment and great joy. We can experience purpose in life. As we mature in our understanding of spiritual gifts and learn to be channels of God's power as he works through them, we are equipped to bear abundant fruit in the kingdom of God.

There is no perfect way for you to organize the ministries, offices, or departments in your place of worship. There is no clear organizational structure in the New Testament. Do you think God did that intentionally so the Church would adapt to different stages, ages, and cultures? In the scriptures, God does give us broad principles, but not narrow rules like in the Old Testament.

Searching the scriptures, we see two general principles about organizing and structuring growth. We will look at various structures of setting up your church. But first, here are some advantages to a simple, *gift-base structure*:

1. *It focuses the church on ministry.* If you stream line your structure, then you can maximize ministry and minimize maintenance. For example, if you cut out about half of your meetings, your church would be more effective. Doing what you can with the faithful few is much more effective that trying to do and be everything to everybody without the available gifts and talents. It will cause the faithful few to burn out.

2. *It makes better use of talent.* When you release people to do what they are good at doing, you will be amazed at how God will multiply. For example, the last thing you want to do is put a person good at lawn maintenance on the kitchen committee. Committees discuss what they want other people to do, ministries just do it.

3. *It builds morale.* A person feels valued when they are liberated to use their skills and talents.

4. *It allows spontaneous growth.* When people see, something missing in your church, they are often revealing their

giftedness. Don't treat it as a criticism, realize that they are revealing their passion.

5. **It promotes growth.** If you allow people to expand and stretch, then you are going to have a creative church. But if you have bureaucracy – "When have always done it this way" – then creative people are going to leave your church

6. **It allows more efficient decision-making.** I have seen churches waste so much time and have so much strife over trivial decisions. I am from a small church and decisions are often based on the popularity of the speaker. Don't allow the one negative person in the church to kill an idea.

As you go through this book looking at helpful suggestions, keep in mind that a simple structure is more stable. The more complicated a structure is, the easier it is to break. If you are just starting your journey, use a simple structure focused on purpose, gifts, and talents. If you are already established your church, here are some suggestions to simplify your structure:

◆ Reduce the number of meetings you have in your church
◆ Reduce the number of items you vote on
◆ Release ministries to make their own decisions
◆ Let your budget determine your priorities. The way you spend your time and your money determines what's important in your church.

This document is intended as a guide for use in forming and organizing your church, leadership staff, and committees. It is based on a two hundred to four hundred member congregation, but its numbers and functions can be expanded or contracted to meet the needs of your particular congregation.

Church Organization

~

What Do I Do?

A Quick Guide to Church Organization

A Brief History

The Place

A critical part of Christianity has been the gathering of people to worship together. By this activity, the 'place' where they worship has become endowed with a symbolic form. To the early Christians the word "church" referred to the act of assembling together rather than to the building itself. It all started after the death, burial and resurrection of Jesus Christ. He told his disciples to wait in the upper room at Jerusalem until they would be endured with power. The picture is a replica model of the upper room. The upper room

Figure 1 According to early Christian tradition, the "upper room" was in the home of Mary the mother of John Mark.

in this case may have only been used because it had adequate space for the apostles to meet. This may have not only given them adequate space but also the privacy that an upper room might have afforded. They needed a place to fellowship, to pray, and be of "one accord," somewhat similar to the upper room experience when Jesus and the disciples met for the Lord's Supper.

The Upper Room, also known as the Cenacle room on Mt Zion in Jerusalem, is where two major events in the early Christian Church are commemorated: The Last Supper and the coming

Figure 2The Cenacle room on Mt Zion in Jerusalem is where two major events in the early Christian Church are commemorated: The Last Supper and the coming of the Holy Spirit on the apostles.

of the Holy Spirit on the apostles. This house was a meeting place for the followers of Jesus inside the city walls of Jerusalem. It was also the house to which Peter went after an angel of the Lord released him from prison.

House-Church.

If Christianity was unrecognized by the Romans, Christians met where they could, mainly in their own homes. The character of these assemblies reflected the nature of their faith during that period, with an

Figure 3 The Dura-Europos house church with chapel area on riight.

emphasis on introspection. The material world was left behind and the real meaning of life was found in the spiritual dimension. Some of these houses or worship were entirely converted into places of worship—*House Church.* The Dura-Europos in Syria is one of the earliest known churches in a normal domestic house converted for worship sometime between 233 and 256, when the town was abandoned after conquest by the Persians.

Popular Types of House Churches

A cell or fellowship group. Cell groups meet together in a member's home primarily for prayer, study and fellowship. They usually have a leader and may also meet corporately with other cell groups from a larger church.

A new traditional church. The pastor of a new church plant may conduct meetings in a member's home until they can afford a permanent facility.

19

An organic house church. This type of church meets in various places, not just houses. The community center, the cafeteria of a public school, or a county auditorium has provided a place for many congregations to hold worship services. The organic house churches are sometimes called organic, simple, or relational church. Emphasis is placed on developing a spontaneous, face-to-face community.

Thinking about starting a house church? Make sure you are doing it for the right reasons. Never start any type of ministry out of frustration, bitterness or anger. If you are patient, God will lead you to the right body of believers.

Over time, the Christian church and faith grew more organized. In 313 AD, the Emperor Constantine issued the Edict of Milan, which accepted Christianity: 10 years later, it had become the official religion of the Roman Empire.

Rome Becomes Christian and Constantine Builds Churches

By the beginning of the fourth century Christianity was a growing mystery religion in the cities of the Roman world. It was attracting converts from different social levels. Christian theology and art was enriched through the cultural interaction with the Greco-Roman world. But Christianity would be radically transformed through the actions of a single man—Constantine.

The "House Church" quickly became an immaculate structure to compare to the other temples throughout the Roman Empire by public cults in defining civic identity. So it was natural for Constantine to want to construct edifices in honor of Christianity. He built churches in Rome including the Church of St. Peter, he built churches in the Holy Land, most notably the Church of the Nativity in Bethlehem and the Church of the Holy Sepulcher in Jerusalem, and he built churches in his newly-constructed capital of Constantinople. Take a look at a few.

The Basilica. The number of Christian worshippers increased gradually over the first few centuries with a substantial increase corresponding to the establishment of Christianity as the state religion of the Roman Empire. Congregations soon outgrew the meeting halls of the House-Churches and so began to create buildings specifically suited to hold their worship. The interior focus of the House-Church was transformed to an emphasis on the artwork of the inner surfaces of the building and a careful introduction of natural light to the interior. See St. Peter's Basilica

Figure 4 Main façade and dome of St. Peter's Basilica seen from St. Peter's square

The Monastery. With the fall of Rome and the rise of Christianity, the importance of temporal political power and the material world was subordinated to the belief in a heavenly and eternal king. The physical characteristics of the architecture reflected this shift. The monastery was a self-sufficient and walled entity protected from within by the experience of the existence of God and from without by symbolic enclosure and solidity.

Figure 5 The Tatev Monastery complex and its fortifications

The Romanesque and Gothic Churches. The notion of God as a continuous presence found architectural expression in an increased emphasis on verticality in the nave of the church. In the Gothic cathedral, God's presence is immediate and, through the cathedral, He communicates very directly with mankind. For the medieval Christian community, the architecture of the cathedral made manifest God's order on earth. Each stone of the

22

building's structure was carved to represent a piece of that order.

Figure 6 Revelation of God in a discrete location, in Romanesque and Gothic cathedrals was symbolized by a verticality that is extended into the entire nave.

Faith was a precondition in which reason could exist. It was, therefore, through the cathedral that meaning could be brought into the lives of men. The congregations and church officials were keenly aware of this emphasis which clarifies the dominance of the cathedral over the village or landscape within which it is set.

The Renaissance. The Renaissance was characterized by an increased faith in mankind as God's creation and therefore as a manifestation of his wisdom. Government, as a manifestation of man's power of reason, emerged as a separate entity from the church. In this age of investigation and discovery, men sought to integrate a realistic approach to nature with an idea of divine cosmic order. As in other ages the church sought to represent this search in the architectural

23

expression of their building. Interior and exterior space was clearly defined and design of these areas was carved out with an emphasis on mathematic geometry, a symbol of man's reason expressing God's order

Figure 7 Florence Cathedral (Cathedral of Santa Maria)

The Church in America.

America is an eclectic accumulation of buildings and denominations. Everything from the house church to the store front church to the mega church. According to quora.com1, the estimated number of church buildings accommodating Christian congregations is approximately 37 million. That's one for every 65 people. The same website indicates that there are 34,000 Christian

[1] https://www.quora.com/

denominations in the world (we'll get back to that in a bit).

These buildings are often called "Storefront Churches" because they are buildings that were previously commercial properties that have been converted to a religious use. Often, the inside of the building was converted by putting in chairs and a makeshift pulpit. The storefront church sometimes serves as a hub for many poor African Americans to see leadership in an all-black area.

Figure 8 Greek Orthodox Church, between a restaurant and a hardware store in an ethnically mixed neighborhood in Queens, New York City

"The Mega-Churches of today hold a strong influence on the general opinion of mainstream America. Followers look for daily guidance from pastors and heads of ministries on the best way to live their lives and raise their families. A megachurch is defined by the Hartford Institute as any Protestant Christian church having 2,000 or more people in average weekend attendance.

Figure 9 Lakewood Church in Huston TX seats 45,000

However, size alone is an insufficient characterization of this distinctive religious reality. The megachurch is a new structural and spiritual organization unlike any other. In order to understand fully the dynamics of megachurches, they must be seen as a collective social phenomenon rather than as individual anomalous moments of spectacular growth or uniquely successful spiritual entrepreneurial ventures.

Although variations exist, most megachurches have a similar identifiable pattern and share a common set of organizational and leadership dynamics. The rise of hundreds of these large churches in the last several decades implies that this new pattern of congregational life has a particular resonance to and fit with changes in modern American society and culture, lives of its members, and its relationship to modern society.

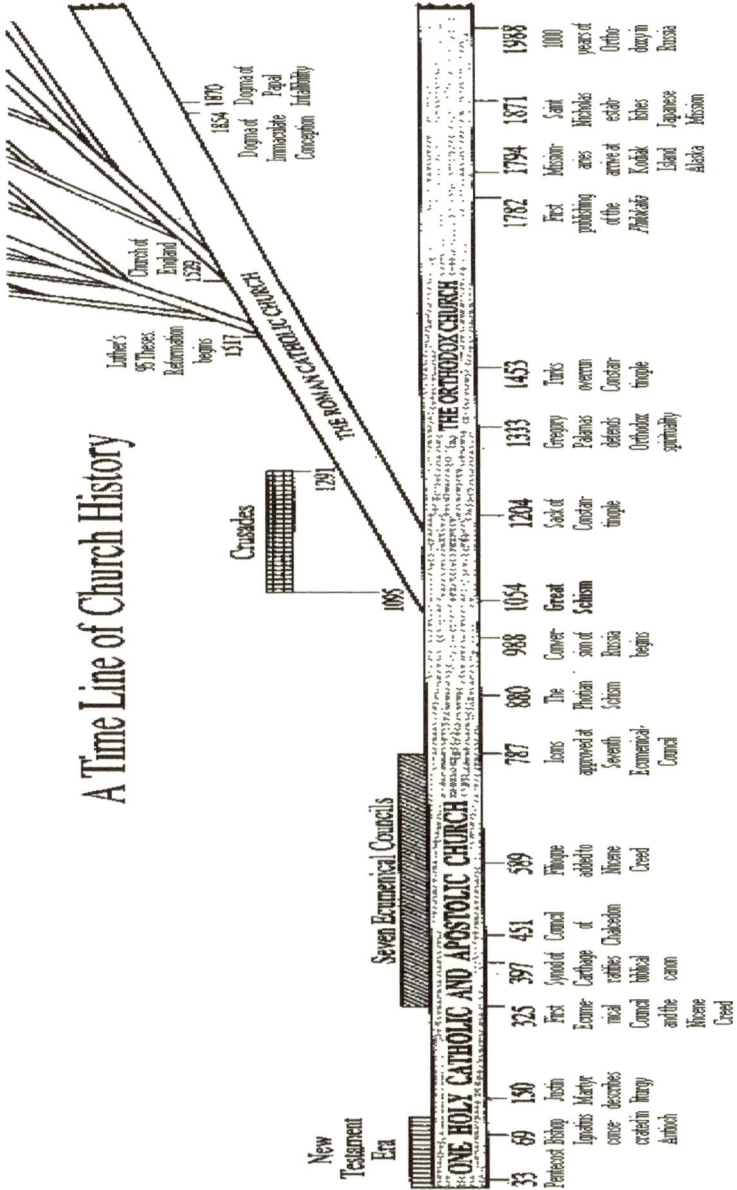

Figure 10 History of the church timeline[ii]
See More at Christianity in View[2]

Chapter 1 How to Start A Church

Except the Lord build the house, they
labour in vain that build it: except the
Lord keep the city, the watchman
waketh but in vain.
~Psalm 127:1 KJV~

The first thing in establishing any organization is spiritual guidance—especially starting a church. If you turn to God's word for guidance, you will never go wrong. Ephesians 4[3] tells us of some of the gifts that God gave to the church for the perfecting of the saints, for the work of the ministry, and for the edifying of the body of Christ. Gifts of the Spirit are special abilities provided by the Holy Spirit to Christians for the purpose of building up the body of Christ. The list of spiritual gifts in 1 Corinthians 12:8-10 includes wisdom, knowledge, faith, healing, miracles, prophecy, discerning of spirits, speaking in tongues, and interpretation of tongues. Similar lists appear in Ephesians 4:7-13 and Romans 12:3-8. We will take a look at these spiritual gifts later on.

The second thing in establishing any organization is the legality of your intentions. A church is a spiritual community that comes together in common fellowship. If you're dissatisfied with your local options and have a group of like-minded thinkers and believers, you may be interested in branching out on your own to worship in your own way. Where to start? You can

---

[2] http://christianityinview.com/timeline.html
[3] https://www.blueletterbible.org/kjv/eph/4/11/s_1101011

learn to begin the early informal processes and plan for an incorporated community, apply for legal status, and expand your church in the community. Here are some suggestions in the form of a step-by-step process.

Look for the Spiritual Gifts

The gifts of the Spirit are simply God enabling believers to do what He has called us to do. 2 Peter 1:3 says, "His divine power has given us everything we need for life and godliness through our knowledge of him who called us by his own glory and goodness." The gifts of the Holy Spirit are part of the "everything we need" to fulfill His purposes for our lives.

Are spiritual gifts the best sign of spirituality? No! Christ-like maturity is primarily indicated by the manifestation of the Fruit of the Spirit, not by the presence of spiritual gifts (Galatians 5:22-23).

God may choose to shine forth in a spiritually immature baby Christian. However, that does not make the baby spiritual. A spiritual child may say excitedly, "I got the gift of tongues last night and now I'm spiritual!" But, Jesus said: "For by their fruit you shall know them" (Matthew 7:16). Satan can imitate and counterfeit spiritual gifts, but he is baffled in trying to imitate the Fruit of the Spirit.

The Holy Spirit distributes the gifts of the Spirit as He sees fit (1 Corinthians 12:7-11). God does not want us to be ignorant of how He wants us to serve Him. However, it is very easy for us to get caught up in what spiritual gift we have and then only serve God in that area of ministry. That is not how it works. God calls us to obediently serve Him. He will equip us with whatever gifts of the Spirit we need to accomplish the task or tasks He has called us to. Yes, God calls some to be teachers and gives them the gift of teaching, but that does not excuse the person from serving God in other ways as well. Is it beneficial to know what spiritual gifts God has given you? Of course, it is. Is it wrong to focus so much on spiritual gifts that we miss other opportunities to serve God? Yes!

That is why a church needs pastors, teachers, helpers, servants, administrators, those with great faith, etc. All of the gifts of the Holy Spirit working together are needed to produce the full potential of the church. With that being said, there is some controversy as to the precise nature of each of the gifts of the Spirit, but here is a list of spiritual gifts and their basic definitions.

- ◆ The gift of wisdom seems to be the proper use of the facts and the ability to make decisions and give guidance that is according to God's will.
- ◆ The gift of knowledge is the accumulations of facts and the ability to have an in-depth understanding of a spiritual issue or situation.
- ◆ The gift of faith is being able to trust God and encourage others to trust God, no matter the circumstances.
- ◆ The gift of healing is the miraculous ability to use God's healing power to restore a person who is sick, injured, or suffering.
- ◆ The gift of miracles is being able to perform signs and wonders that give authenticity to God's Word and the Gospel message.

- The gift of prophecy is being able to proclaim a message from God.
- The gift of discerning spirits is the ability to determine whether or not a message, person, or event is truly from God.
- The gift of tongues is the ability to speak in a foreign language that you do not have knowledge of, in order to communicate with someone who speaks that language.
- The gift of interpreting tongues is the ability to translate the tongues speaking and communicate it back to others in your own language.
- The gift of administration is being able to keep things organized and in accordance with God's principles.
- The gift of helps is always having the desire and ability to help others, to do whatever it takes to get a task accomplished.

Be sure not to confuse these gifts of the spirit with talents. A person (regardless of his belief in God or in Christ) is given a natural talent as a result of a combination of genetics (some have natural ability in music, art, or mathematics) and surroundings (growing up in a musical family will aid one in developing a talent for music), or because God desired to endow certain individuals with certain talents.

This may be hard for some of you to understand, but as Paul said, consider what I say and may God give you the understanding. Spiritual gifts are given to all believers by the Holy Spirit (Romans 12:3, 6) at the time they place their faith in Christ. *"For the gifts and calling of God are without repentance." ~Romans 11:29 KJV.* The Holy Spirit gives to the new believer the spiritual gift(s)
31

He desires the believer to have (1 Corinthians 12:11).

Beginning Fellowship

As you develop friendly associations with people of like interests, look for the gifts of the spirit as you follow these steps of beginning fellowship.

Step 1: Start a home spiritual discussion group. Before you attempt to file for non-profit status and make your church official, it's best to establish a somewhat sizable and united fellowship of people with similar beliefs to undergo the process together. Start talking with like-minded people and getting together on a regular basis.
 ◆ The IRS requires you to have three founding members who are not related by blood or marriage.
 ◆ You would want to seek out

Step 2: Define the scope of the church. You can establish a church at varying levels and the better you define your aims for the church, the easier it will be to establish your tax-exempt status. Establishing a ministry, for example, is somewhat different than forming a corporately structured church, housed in its own building. Consider:
 ◆ Your possible membership. How many do you reasonably expect?
 ◆ Your location. Where will you worship?
 ◆ Your commitment. Will this be a part-time job, or a full-time calling?

◆ Your financial aims. Will your church collect funds? How? How much will be necessary?

Step 3: Draft church bylaws and a statement of belief. Why are you starting a church? What core beliefs will govern your ministry? What distinguishes your church in terms of doctrine and creed? These are questions to take up in a statement of belief. Think of this as the "Declaration of Independence" for your church.

◆ To form a religious organization, you need to also establish a series of bylaws by which your organization will be governed. Think of this as the rule book for your church's operations. Will you perform weddings and funerals? Under what protocol? What community outreach programs will your church participate in?

◆ Sample outlines of bylaws are available online that you can use and modify for your purposes.

Step 4: Assign corporate officers. You'll need corporate officers, a board of directors, and a membership to file for incorporation with the state. Make sure ahead of time you've got willing participants to fulfill the various procedural and accounting roles necessary to make a church run smoothly.[4]

◆ These roles will be different than church staff. You don't necessarily need to think about janitorial and secretarial roles just yet, but make sure you've got some idea of the board of directors, visiting and youth ministry, music,

---

[4] http://www.themonastery.org/starting-a-church/your-own-church

33

and fundraising. The decision-making players need to be in place before you move forward.

Step 5: Name your church. A commonly overlooked step. Give some thought to naming your church something distinctive, unique, and descriptive of your niche in the ministry. Also make sure you're not repeating a commonly-used name.

Make it Legal-Forming a Non-Profit

This is one area where it is good to have fellowship with people with the gift of administration.

Step 1: Consult a lawyer. It's perfectly possible to apply for incorporation and tax exemption without consulting a lawyer, but it is not the most straightforward process in the world and it would be beneficial to consult a lawyer after preparing the paperwork to the best of your abilities. Always get your work double-checked, but try to save money by doing as much of it as possible yourself.

Step 2: Understand the guidelines and rules of tax-exemption and structure your corporation accordingly. Your church must satisfy the following requirements:
- ◆ The organization must be organized and operated exclusively for religious, educational, scientific, or other charitable purposes.
- ◆ Net earnings may not go to the benefit of any private individual or shareholder.

♦ No substantial part of its activity may be attempting to influence legislation and may not intervene in political campaigns.

♦ The organization's purposes and activities may not be illegal or violate fundamental public policy.

Step 3: Get incorporation documents in your state. Obtain the documents of incorporation from the Business Bureau in your state. If you've already configured your corporate offices, composed a belief statement, and meet the proper requirements, you're halfway there.

♦ Get a few copies of the same documents to practice on. If you mess up, just start over.

Step 4: Confirm your 501(c) (3) status. At the regional IRS office, ask for a formal review of your documentation and a notice of exemption. As long as you meet the requirements, all churches should automatically qualify for 501 status without more action.

♦ It's not necessary to take any extra step to ensure tax exemption. However, many churches take the extra step of IRS recognition to ensure to church leaders, members, and contributors that the church is recognized, exempt, and in good legal stead with the state. This is especially important when a church is just starting out and hoping to promote legitimacy.

♦ You can also fill out IRS form 1023, found at: http://www.irs.gov/pub/irs-pdf/f1023.pdf

Step 5: Fill out the SS4 form with the IRS to get an Employer Identification Number (EIN). Regardless of whether or not you hire employees, it's important to acquire an EIN from the IRS to allow you to open a church bank account and also to file returns with the IRS.

◆ Find this form here: http://www.irs.gov/pub/irs-pdf/fss4.pdf

Step 6: Open a church bank account. Use your EIN and other documentation to open an account used specifically for the church's funds.[2] To open an account, you'll typically be asked to provide:

◆ Proof of your EIN
◆ Photo ID, and social security numbers of the principal signers
◆ Master list of the church's board of directors and corporate officers

Building Your Church

Step 1: Find an appropriate place to worship. Eventually, as your church grows, you'll probably want to take it out of the living room and into the world. Find an appropriate location that will be easy to grow in, and easy for new followers to find and make it to. Find somewhere you can afford and take the time to organize and decorate it according to your particular aesthetics and core beliefs.

Step 2: Develop a compelling message. Why should people come listen to your interpretation of your common beliefs? What do you bring to the table? How can you enrich their spiritual life in a way that other churches and communities can't? These are important questions to consider as you build your program and begin holding services. Address basic questions:

- Who will preach?
- What sort of music will be included?
- How will a service be structured?

Step 3: Consider joining a district office in your denomination. If you're within the umbrella of a pre-existing denomination, consider joining up with the regional office and sending representatives to the yearly meetings in your area. This can be a good way to make connections in your area and attract new members.

- In general, be careful about "leeching" off the memberships of established churches in your area. It's probable that people who attend your church might be dissatisfied with their options, and you should create a welcoming space for those people.
- However, don't actively preach against other local churches, or attend their services and sow dissent. Create harmony rather than strife.

Step 4: Establish your unique personality and presence in the community. When you're first getting started and have built a small group of followers and regular attendees, set a regular time for services and actively seek new members.

- Hold informal functions like cookouts and street festivals to attract neighbors and other potential members, and maintain an open door policy to build your church.

- Regularly hold open-house events to attract new members. Advertise your church regularly in local weeklies and maintain an open-door policy to cultivate a welcoming presence. If you want to gain a membership and a solid community, get the word out.

Step 5: Include a time of fellowship and get to know your members. A church without a community is just a building. People will continue to come if they feel welcome and cared for, and you want to make sure that your church is a place people feel free to worship and come together.
- Take a personal interest in each person and their family.
- Visit or call during the time between the meetings, taking an honest interest in their beliefs, their lives, and their needs from the church.
- If there are members (especially the young people) that are willing to contact members that were not present in service, let them set it up to call, text, tweet, or Facebook them.

Step 6: As the group grows, make decisions together as a group. As a founding member, you may have a great idea about having a Christian Metal festival with a pop-up skate park, but your congregation may not be thrilled about the idea.
- Discuss it openly and come together to make the decision. It's not your job to push legislation through--it's your job to build up a community that worships together.
- If funding or charitable needs increase find ways to encourage giving in your church.

Summary ~ to Start Your Church

Establish Incorporation:[5] The articles of incorporation give you a strong legal shield, ensuring your limited legal liability, and protecting you and your members. This document should reflect your vision and mission, give you the ability to license and ordain ministers of the gospel and that serve as the legal birth of your organization.

Obtain Federal Employer Identification Number (FEIN): the information you need to open a church bank account, enabling you to take tax-deductible tithes and offerings. This number is used to identify your corporation and is needed for business and federal purposes. This number may also be known as a Tax ID Number.

Create Bylaws: Other than the Scriptures, the bylaws* are the most important document in your church. Bylaws empowers you to protect your vision, your ministry, and your members, adopting the governmental structure that reflects your ministry structure and allowing the pastor's vision to be kept clear.

Establish Policy: Develop essential policies that help establish and protect your board of directors and those helping lead your ministry.

Obtain 501(c)(3) Tax-Exempt Status: 501c3 status allows donors to receive a tax deduction, provides grant funding eligibility for the nonprofit, lower postage rates, and increased credibility within the community. View Video: https://www.irsvideos.gov/CharitiesAndNonProfits

---

[5] https://www.irs.gov/charities-non-profits/exempt-organizations-continuing-professional-education-technical-instruction-program

39

How to Pay Church Workers

Church jobs are good choices for individuals who want to combine their careers and faith. Churches employ ministers, choir directors, bookkeepers and other workers such as administrators. Pay typically is not that much for the majority of church staff jobs, but the positions provide plenty of opportunities for offering spiritual and economic relief to individuals and communities.

Clergy are the religious leaders within the church such as ministers, pastors and priests. The Bureau of Labor Statistics[6] (BLS) provides salary information for these workers but does not break down earnings according to denomination or leader title. They show that, based on 2017 data, the average annual wage for a member of the clergy was $50,800, or roughly $24.43 per hour. The range of wages, however, is $25,430 to $80,060, or $12.23 to $38.49 per hour. According to BLS, some other average annual pay scales as of May, 2017 are:

- ◆ Music Directors $50,590
- ◆ Musicians & Singers $37,690
- ◆ Church Clerks/Secretary $41,110
- ◆ Usher/Lobby Attendants $22,580
- ◆ Kitchen/Food Service $31,690

Keep in mind that this is the average and full time positions.

Payscale[7] reports more specific salary information for members of the clergy. As of 2017,

---

[6] https://www.bls.gov/oes/2017/may/oes212011.htm
[7] https://www.payscale.com/research/US/Job=Ministry_Director/Salary

40

ministry directors make $40,207. Youth ministers earn $35,646, which is roughly equivalent to the wage of youth pastors ($37,113). Associate pastors earn $46,258. Senior pastors make the highest wages, which average $57,849. According to Payscale annual pay for 2017 were:

- ◆ Music Directors $38,983
- ◆ Musicians & Singers $39,888
- ◆ Church Clerks/Secretary $27,263
- ◆ Usher/Lobby Attendants $21,862
- ◆ Kitchen/Food Service $22,792

Self-employed or Employee?

Ministers usually have a dual tax status and should be treated as employees for income tax purposes and self-employed for Social Security purposes with respect to their ministerial earnings.

Sometimes it's difficult for churches to decide if other paid workers are employees or independent contractors. Employers should generally err on the side of treating workers as employees if they aren't sure. If a church treats a worker as an independent contractor and the IRS later reclassifies that worker as an employee, the church could face substantial fines.

For more information about how the IRS decides if a worker is an independent contractor or employee, see IRS Publication 15-A[8], Employer's Supplemental Tax Guide (Supplement to Publication 15 (Circular E), Employer's Tax Guide), on the IRS Web site at http://www.irs.gov.[9]

---

[8] https://www.irs.gov/pub/irs-pdf/p15a.pdf
[9] https://www.irs.gov/publications/p15

These facts suggest to the IRS that a worker is an employee instead of self-employed:

- The worker is required to follow an employer's instructions about when, where, and how to work.
- The worker receives on-the-job training from an experienced employee.
- The worker is expected to perform the services personally, and not use a substitute.
- The employer, rather than the worker, hires and pays any assistants.
- The worker has a continuing working relationship with the employer.
- The employer establishes set hours of work.
- The worker is expected to work full time (more than 20 hours per week).
- The work is done on the employer's premises.
- The worker must submit regular oral or written reports to the employer.
- The employer reimburses the worker's business expenses.
- The employer furnishes the worker's tools, supplies and equipment.
- The worker does not work for other employers.
- The worker does not advertise his or her services to the general public.

Workers don't have to meet all of these factors to be considered an employee. If they meet most of them, the IRS will consider them to be employees. That's why churches should treat workers as employees rather than independent contractors if they are in doubt.

Considerations: The size of a church greatly impacts the salary available for staff members. The
42

larger the church, in general, the more responsibilities staff members have. For example, a senior pastor at a church with a congregation of 1,000 may preside over just one or two services, while a senior pastor in a mega church may be giving services every day. Similarly, a choir director in a small church may have only one choir to oversee, while one in a large church may have as many as five or six. This translates to more hours worked, which increases salaries. Location also can be a factor, as with other jobs.

A very helpful guide to a pastors' and Christian church salaries can be found at:

- Average Pastor Salary
  https://www.payscale.com/research/US/Job=Pastor/Salary
- Average Christian Church Salary
  https://www.payscale.com/research/US/Employer=Christian_Church/Salary

Use this publication to aid you and your church leaders in organizing for the effectiveness of ministry. You will find suggestions on how to make and keep your church a legal non-profit organization, in organizing its staff and leaders, and in writing job descriptions for the staff members, committees and officers. This publication is intended to serve only as a guide, with each church developing its unique organization.

The organizational structure of a particular church is not always clear. Sometimes the veteran membership have a difficult time knowing what to do or where they fit in the church body not to mention new members.

One of the most important topics for churches serious about being effective in their mission, is church structure and leadership. Did you know that in most churches, as the church grows the organization of the church actually begins to hinder further growth? The dynamics of growth (such as needing to accommodate more people, reacting to the increased number of problems, making decisions on the run, stretching budget dollars, and scheduling more events, meetings, etc.) demand a streamlined organization and leadership empowered to dream, strategize, decide and move ahead.

Stories are often told of staff (either paid or unpaid) wanting to maximize opportunities by being creative but being stymied by needing numerous committee approvals. The youth pastor wants to incorporate a praise dance group after hearing negative comments about the lack of engagement of the young people from parents new to the church. A praise dance team (a trend in youth ministry) would be a nice touch and relatively inexpensive; plus letting the young people do it would be a good character building project. But a member of the youth committee is out of town, the church program committee has a different idea, and the budget committee wants to wait until the next fiscal year. So nothing happens. Families eventually leave. You can avoid that problem with a church organization chart which shows how church leaders, officers, members and volunteers are organized to fulfill their duties.

Leadership of a church must always be asking themselves, how can we:

◆ Be ahead of the growth curve of the church
◆ Simplify structure to enhance growth rather than hinder it
◆ Avoid duplication of responsibility and authority;
◆ Avoid bottlenecks
◆ Quicken the decision making process
◆ Trust staff to act without prior approval
◆ Delegate responsibility to the "front lines"
◆ Empower ministry yet maintain appropriate accountability.

A church has many different areas of work to be done. To accomplish this work, it may choose to organize itself as follows:

◆ Pastor and Staff
◆ Deacons
◆ Church Leadership Team (Church Council)
◆ General Church Officers
    o Moderator
    o Clerk
    o Treasurer

- o Trustees
- ◆ Church Program Organizations
- ◆ Standing Committees
- ◆ Special Committees
- ◆ Age group and other Ministry Councils

The main thing to remember is that you can make it as simple or as complicated as you want. I suggest to keep it simple.

A healthy Church can operate with a poor governance model. It's also true that a church can follow a great model and still be unhealthy. However, if the goal is to remove roadblocks to effective ministry, empower leaders to lead as they have been charged by the Scriptures, and unleash the greatest number of people in meaningful ministry, then structure matters — a great deal.

To visualize the organization of your own church, start with some of these examples. To help you, Lucid chart has a website where you can sign up for a free[10] tool to create your own organizational chart. In the beginning, you may want to keep it very simple. Alternative A is a very simple organizational chart. As your membership and willing workers grow, you may graduate to Alternative B, Alternative C, or some of the other multi-staff organization charts.

---

[10] https://www.lucidchart.com/pages/templates/org-chart/church-org-chart-template

Alternate A

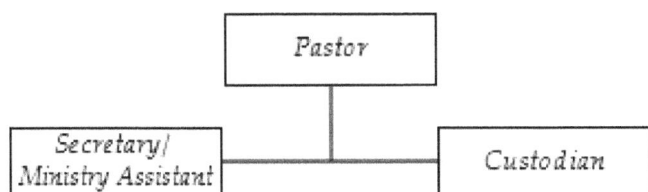

Pastor

Secretary/Ministry Assistant   Custodian

Alternate B

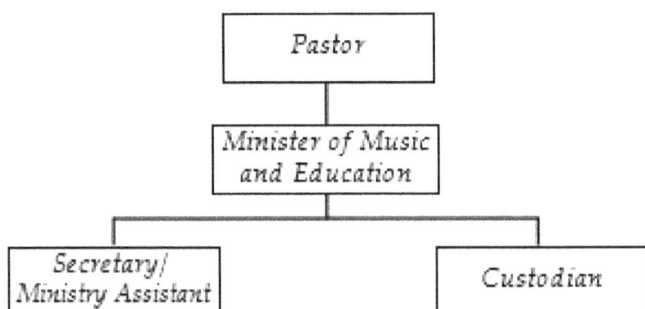

Pastor

Minister of Music and Education

Secretary/Ministry Assistant   Custodian

Alternate C

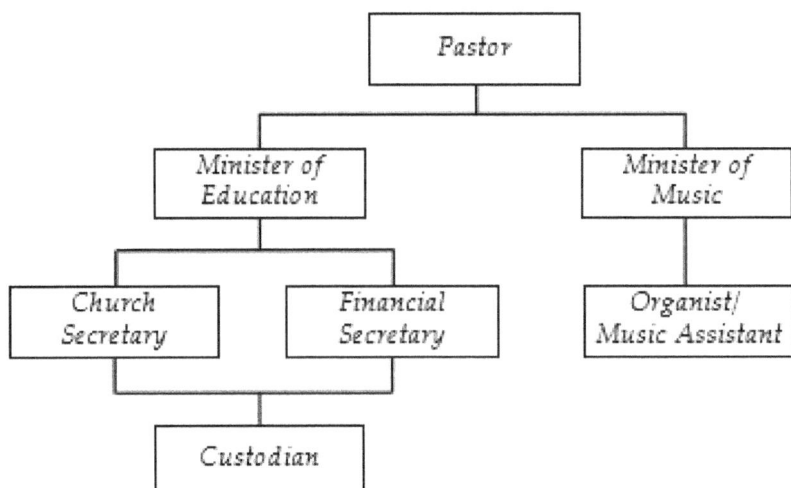

Pastor

Minister of Education   Minister of Music

Church Secretary   Financial Secretary   Organist/Music Assistant

Custodian

SAMPLE MULTI-STAFF CHURCH
ORGANIZATION CHART

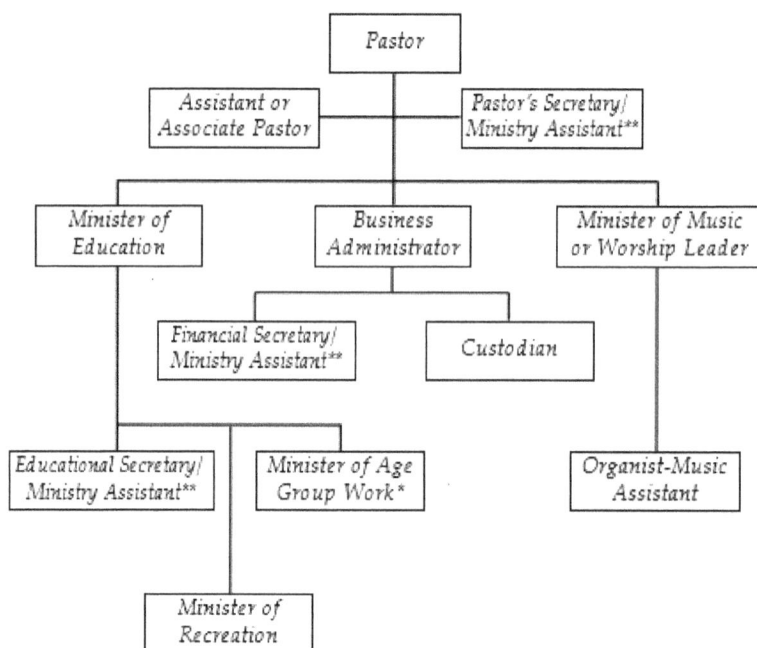

```
                          ┌──────────────┐
                          │    Pastor    │
                          └──────────────┘
  ┌──────────────┐                        ┌──────────────────────┐
  │ Assistant or │                        │ Pastor's Secretary/  │
  │Associate Pastor│                      │ Ministry Assistant** │
  └──────────────┘                        └──────────────────────┘

┌──────────────┐      ┌──────────────┐      ┌──────────────────┐
│ Minister of  │      │   Business   │      │ Minister of Music│
│  Education   │      │ Administrator│      │ or Worship Leader│
└──────────────┘      └──────────────┘      └──────────────────┘

        ┌──────────────────────┐   ┌──────────────┐
        │ Financial Secretary/ │   │  Custodian   │
        │ Ministry Assistant** │   └──────────────┘
        └──────────────────────┘

┌──────────────────────┐  ┌──────────────┐   ┌──────────────┐
│ Educational Secretary/│  │Minister of Age│  │Organist-Music│
│ Ministry Assistant** │  │ Group Work*  │   │  Assistant   │
└──────────────────────┘  └──────────────┘   └──────────────┘

        ┌──────────────┐
        │ Minister of  │
        │  Recreation  │
        └──────────────┘
```

*Figure 6*Age group ministers may include minister to single adults, minister of adult work, minister of children's work, minister of preschool work, minister of youth (students).*

Example of a church organizational chart.

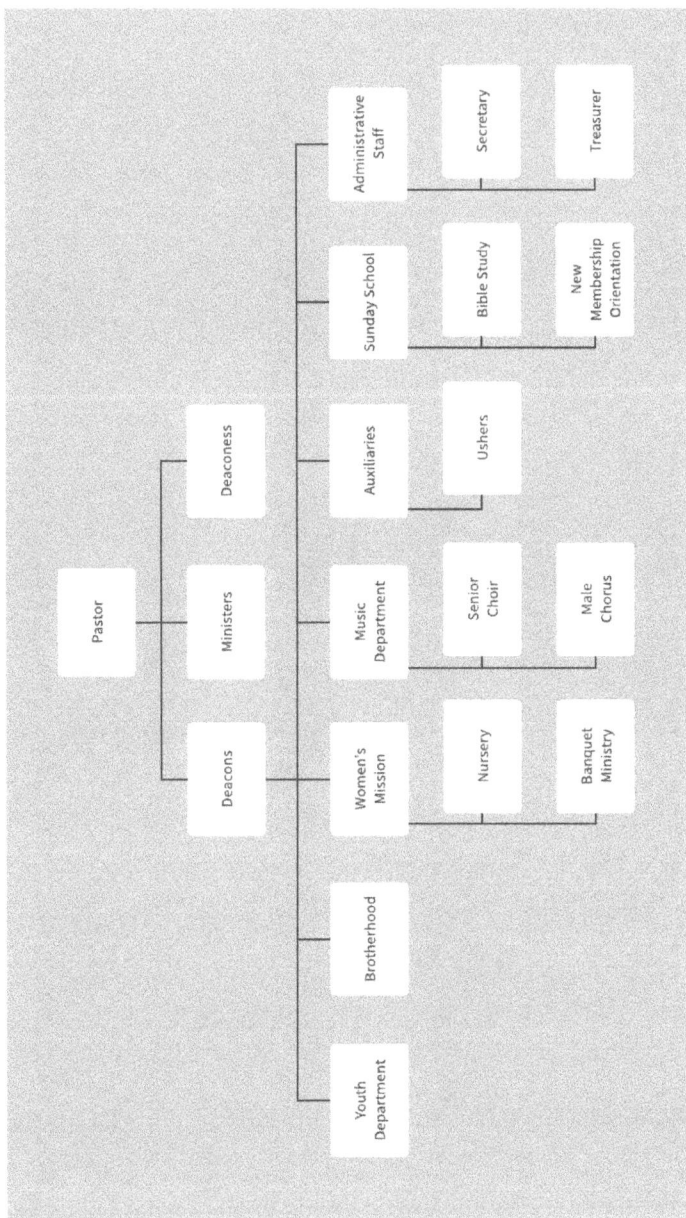

Pastor
- Deaconess
- Ministers
- Deacons
- Administrative Staff
  - Secretary
  - Treasurer
- Sunday School
  - Bible Study
  - New Membership Orientation
- Auxiliaries
  - Ushers
- Music Department
  - Senior Choir
  - Male Chorus
- Women's Mission
  - Nursery
  - Banquet Ministry
- Brotherhood
- Youth Department

Basic Church Programs

Although this book is non-denominational, six programs, common in Southern Baptist churches, have a primary task in the church. Each program develops its organization and seeks to involve the congregation in its work. These organizations are the foundation of the church structure, and thus are called basic church programs. Each one interprets and undergirds the local church and the denomination.

As you can see by the titles of these programs, it is common in the south and some other cultures for churches to have separate programs for men and women. Some go as far as to seat men on one side of the church and women on the other. Let the Bible speak to this situation.

"Then Peter opened his mouth and said, of a truth, I perceive that God is no respecter of persons."
~ Acts 10:34 KJV.

Another scripture says

"There is neither Jew nor Greek, there is neither bond nor free, there is neither male nor female for ye are all one in Christ Jesus"
~ Galatians 3:28 KJV[11]

---

[11]
https://www.blueletterbible.org/search/search.cfm?Criteria=neither+male+female&t=KJV#s=s_primary_0_1

Bible Teaching (Sunday school)
◆ Reach persons of all ages for Bible study
◆ Teach the Bible as the life-changing Word of God
◆ Witness to persons about Christ and church membership
◆ Minister to persons in need in the church and community

Discipleship Training
◆ Reach persons for discipleship training
◆ Orient new members for discipleship, personal and family ministry
◆ Equip church members for discipleship, personal and family ministry
◆ Teach theology, doctrine, ethics, history and church polity
◆ Train church leaders for their tasks

Music Ministry
◆ Provide musical experiences in worship services
◆ Provide church music education for all ages
◆ Lead the church to witness and minister through music
◆ Assist church programs in use of and support with music

Men's Ministry/Brotherhood
◆ Engage men and boys in mission activities
◆ Teach, pray for and give to missions
◆ Develop personal ministry for men and boys
◆ Provide opportunities for fellowship for men and boys

Women's Ministry/Woman's Missionary Union
- Engage women and girls in mission activities
- Teach, pray for and give to missions
- Develop personal ministry for women and girls
- Provide opportunities for fellowship for women and girls

Pastoral Ministries (Pastoral Staff and Deacons)
- Lead the church to accomplish its mission
- Proclaim the gospel to believers and unbelievers
- Care for church members and persons in the community
- Provide servant leadership for the total church ministry

Church Leadership Team
(Sometimes Called Church Council or Board)

The Church Leadership Team serves the congregation as a planning and advisory organization. The church should establish the membership, terms of service and duties of the Team. It is important that the Team focus on the total work of the church. The Team does not have authority over the organizations and committees of the church.

Principal Function: To assist the church to fulfill its mission and to coordinate and evaluate its work.

Method of election: Church leaders become members of the Team as set forth in the Bylaws via designated church leadership positions.

Term of office: Corresponds to the term of office in church-related position

Members: The customary members are the pastor (chairperson of the Team), staff members, church program directors, deacon body chairman, committee chairpersons (which committees should be clarified in the Bylaws), and other key leaders deemed necessary.

Duties:
◆ Help the church understand its Biblical mission and define priorities
◆ Guide the church to write mission, vision, and core value statements

- Coordinate studies of the church and community needs
- Recommend to the church an annual calendar of coordinated plans for evangelism, discipleship, fellowship, missions, ministry and worship
- Coordinate the church's schedule of activities, special events, and use of the facilities
- Evaluate progress and priority use of church resources
- Make regular reports to the church • Lead the church to celebrate the victories and blessings from God
- Model for the church cooperation as a basis of church ministry

Note: In larger and mega churches with multiple staff members, the work of the Team is planned, coordinated and evaluated primarily through the staff with input and coordination through program leaders and key committees.

Developing Staff Team Spirit

The responsibility to develop team spirit begins with the pastor. Each staff member has an individual responsibility to do their part in building a strong fellowship and common loyalty shared by the members. Team spirit cannot be manufactured by manipulating other persons, but through love, respect, servant ministry and visionary leadership. Churches need this type of team spirit to experience spiritual health and growth. The following practical and spiritual actions develop team spirit within a church staff.

- ◆ Pray for each other on a regular basis.
- ◆ Keep the lines of communication open with each other.
- ◆ Understand and follow church-approved personnel policies.
- ◆ Understand and follow the lines of supervision and communication.
- ◆ Respect each other as fellow believers and employees.
- ◆ Develop a team spirit based on church mission ("no dream, no team").
- ◆ Confront conflict consistently on an individual and private basis.
- ◆ Develop interpersonal skills such as initiating, diagnosing, listening, communicating, and problem-solving.
- ◆ Require continuing education of all staff members.
- ◆ Conduct regular staff meetings (weekly, semiweekly, monthly, etc.).

- Express appreciation openly and genuinely to each other.
- Grow spiritually to develop right attitudes and motives toward others.
- Conduct ministry planning sessions involving all staff members.
- Plan staff retreats for prayer, sharing, studying, dreaming and team-building.
- Remember the team principle: together everyone accomplishes more.
- Have informal and social gatherings to develop staff relationships and fellowship.
- Desire and develop an atmosphere of love, trust and mutual support.

Content Suggestions for Personnel Policy Handbook

It is good to have a personnel policy handbook or manual that serves as an introduction to the church, and a reference for any questions your staff, employee, or volunteers may have. In addition to informing personnel of their duties, the handbook provides information on key policies, such as benefits, dress code, and work schedules. The personnel handbook should include:

- ◆ Church Employee Categories
  - ○ Called Staff
  - ○ Support Staff
- ◆ Benefits for... –
  - ○ Called Staff – Full/Part-Time
  - ○ Support Staff - Full/Part-Time
- ◆ Employment Procedures Support Staff
- ◆ Termination Procedures
- ◆ Vacations
- ◆ Other Employment and
- ◆ Sick Days Interim Positions
- ◆ Holidays

- ◆ Working Relationships
- ◆ Absences
- ◆ School Attendance
- ◆ Leave of Absence
- ◆ Working Conditions
- ◆ Military Leave
- ◆ Pay Policies
- ◆ Bereavement Leave
- ◆ Leave of Absence
- ◆ Maternity Leave
- ◆ Sexual Harassment
- ◆ Study Leave
- ◆ Probation Period
- ◆ Jury Duty
- ◆ Expenses/Reimbursements

◆ Anniversary
  Recognition

◆ Technology/Equip
  ment

◆ Emergency Leave

Content Suggestions--Personnel File

The employee personnel file is the main employee file that contains the history of the employment relationship from employment application through an exit interview and employment termination documentation.

In some circumstances, personnel files can become evidence in a lawsuit brought against your church by an unhappy former employee or employees. As a result, you should always ensure that certain documents are maintained and updated in your employees' personnel files in order to protect yourself and your congregation.

◆ Application/Resume/Letter of Inquiry
◆ Correspondence/Notes Regarding References
◆ Criminal Background Check (work with minors)
◆ Tests of Job Skills (if applicable)
◆ Job (Position) Description
◆ Offer Letter, Response and Agreements • W-4, 1-9 and Copy of Tax Records
◆ Insurance Application(s) and Information
◆ Annuity Application and Materials
◆ Salary Reduction Agreement
◆ Cover Sheet
◆ Attendance Record
◆ Career Development Plan and Record
◆ Annual Evaluations
◆ Record of Disciplinary Action

- ◆ Letters of Commendation
- ◆ Copies of Insurance Claims Filed
- ◆ Copy of All Policies and Materials Given to Employees • Termination Notice
- ◆ Driver (Transportation) Information (if applicable)

Chapter 3 Job Descriptions Ministry & Staff

A model of church ministerial job descriptions should clearly delineates responsibilities, authority, and lines of accountability. It answers the questions,
◆ Who is responsible for accomplishing the mission of the church?
◆ What authority do they have in determining the means for accomplishing the mission'? And
◆ Who are they accountable to for the actual results?

Now it is time to allow your following to use their spiritual gifts. Here are some sample ministerial functions and responsibilities:[12]

Pastor

Principal Function: The pastor is responsible to the church for proclaiming the gospel of Jesus Christ, for using his/her skills in administrative leadership, for engaging in pastoral care ministries to meet the needs of persons in the church and in the community, and to act as the chief administrator of the ministerial and vocational staff.

Responsibilities:
◆ Set as a guideline of personal behavior the standard required in 1 Timothy 3:1-7 and I Peter 5:1-4.

---

[12] These are suggested titles and responsibilities

- Provide administrative leadership for the total church program.
- Maintain a regular program of study to enable himself to plan and conduct meaningful worship services.
- Prepare for and conduct worship services; lead in the observance of the ordinances; and, lead the church in proclaiming the gospel to the church and community.
- Visit members and prospects and lead the membership in a visitation program.
- Supervise other members of the church staff according to staff organization.
- Conduct premarital, vocational, family, bereavement, counseling sessions, etc., as needed. Advise other professional help when necessary. • Perform wedding ceremonies and conduct funeral services.
- Work with deacons, church officers, and committees in performing assigned responsibilities. Be available for and lead in training as needed.
- Cooperate with and lead the church in cooperating with associational, state, and denominational leaders. Keep the church informed of developments within the denomination.
- Serve as a representative of the church in civic matters.
- Serve as the leader in seeking to win the unsaved and lead the membership in soul-winning training.
- Plan and promote periods of evangelistic emphasis for the unsaved and renewal for the Christians.

- Serve as chairman of the Church Leadership Team (Church Council) in planning, organizing, directing, coordinating and evaluating the total church program.
- Act as moderator for church business meetings, if the bylaws require it.

Associate Pastor

Principal Function: The associate pastor supervises the ministerial staff, gives attention to the administrative details related to programming and aids in all pastoral responsibilities as deemed necessary and/or appropriate by the pastor.

Responsibilities:
- Assist the pastor in the overall programming of the church, aid in special projects, and implement specific assignments by the pastor related to general pastoral activities.
- Maintain clear channels of communication with the pastor to inform the pastor of needs, activities, and/or problems and to receive the pastor's input, insight and affirmation related to plans and decisions.
- Meet regularly with the pastor and ministerial staff for planning, evaluating and coordinating the ministries of the church.
- Supervise and assist the ministerial staff in planning, coordinating and implementing programs related to their areas of responsibility.

- Conduct semiannual reviews of performance based on program objectives and goals.
- Work with the pastor and appropriate committees and other staff members in seeking needed new staff members.
- Work with the staff and congregation to achieve the objectives of the church. • Work with appropriate groups to develop a comprehensive church calendar.
- Organize and oversee a visitation program to include in reach and outreach.
- Direct a program for new member and new Christian orientation

Business Administrator

Principal Function: The business administrator is responsible to the pastor for the accurate accounting and handling of all church finances and for administering the business affairs of the church.

Responsibilities:
◆ Work with the ministerial staff and appropriate church committees in planning, implementing and monitoring the annual church budget.
◆ Establish and maintain an efficient plan of financial record keeping and reporting.
◆ Work with the chairman of the Stewardship Committee in planning and implementing the annual stewardship emphasis.
◆ Direct the maintenance program of the church.
◆ Work with the Missions Committee to establish goals for special mission emphasis.
◆ Report to all committees and staff members the financial status of their particular area of ministry. • Administer church-adopted policies and procedures concerning the use of all church properties and facilities.
◆ Participate in weekly hospital and prospect visitation. • Serve as a resource person in legal and business matters.
◆ Study annually the insurance program and recommend necessary changes.
◆ Maintain church staff personnel, equipment and facilities rec

Minister of Education

Principal Function: The minister of education is responsible to the pastor for the total educational church program in planning, conducting and evaluating a comprehensive Christian education ministry to achieve the mission of the church.

Responsibilities:
◆ Correlate all programs, plans and activities with the staff and church council.
◆ Maintain the church calendar of activities.
◆ Train and work closely with the Nominating Committee in selecting and enlisting qualified leaders for the educational program.
◆ Serve as resource and liaison person for committees related to the educational program.
◆ Plan special emphases in educational programs (i.e. attendance campaigns, leadership recognition, Preparation Week, VBS, promotion, January Bible Study, etc.).
  • Coordinate the production of church publications.
◆ Develop special educational/training projects such as camps, retreats and seminars.
◆ Lead in regular education program organization planning meetings.
◆ Lead in choosing and securing the most suitable educational and curriculum materials available.
◆ Supervise appropriate church staff members.

Church Clerk

Principal Function: The Church Clerk is responsible for recording, processing and maintaining accurate records of all church business meeting transactions. Sometimes along with possible church office personnel they are responsible for all accurate church membership changes and communication of membership transitions. The Church Clerk may also be asked to keep the minutes in the Church Administrative Business Council meetings.

Responsibilities:
- Keep an accurate record (minutes) of all regular and special business meetings and transactions made and approved by the church.
- Present the minutes of prior meetings(s) at each business meeting for church approval.
- Provide clerical assistance during the invitation period of the worship services for new members, re-dedications and other decisions.
- Maintain an accurate record of the church membership, including the dates of admission, termination and method of joining the church.
- Correspond with other churches for membership changes.
- Preserve records for church history.
- Prepare the Annual Church Profile.
- Assist in preparation of the agenda for business meeting(s).
- Work with church officers and trustees in preparation of legal documents.

Minister of Music

Principal Function: The minister of music is responsible to the pastor for the total music ministry of the church. Direct the planning, organizing, conducting and evaluating of a comprehensive music program in preparing groups, soloists and choirs for internal and external ministry.

Responsibilities:
- ◆ Work with the ministerial staff on special music needs in the total church program.
- ◆ Supervise the work of the music ministry staff.
- ◆ Work with the nominating committee to enlist and train leaders for the music ministry.
- ◆ Work with the pastor in selecting music for regular and special worship services – including weddings, funerals and special projects.
- ◆ Coordinate the music program with the organizational calendar and emphases of the church.
- ◆ Participate in regular hospital and prospect visitation.
- ◆ Monitor the purchasing, maintenance and replacement of all music-related equipment, supplies and instruments.
- ◆ Keep informed on music methods, materials, promotion and administration.
- ◆ Prepare an annual music budget for approval and administer the budget.

- ◆ Direct congregational singing at all regularly scheduled worship services.
- ◆ Plan and arrange an "Order of Service" for worship services.
- ◆ Cooperate with associational and state leaders in promoting activities of mutual interest.

Music Assistant (Keyboard, Piano, Organ)

Music Ministry Assistant

Principal Function: The music secretary serves as ministry assistant to the minister of music and performs general office duties related to the music ministry.

Responsibilities:
◆ Type all correspondence for the minister of music.
◆ Record messages for minister of music.
◆ Serve as receptionist for the music department.
◆ Maintain office files and records.
◆ Maintain music library.
◆ Order and catalog new music as needed.
◆ Accept additional responsibilities as needed.

Keyboard/Organist/Pianist (Music Assistant)

Principal Function: The organist (pianist)/music assistant is responsible to the minister of music for serving at the organ/piano and assisting in the music ministry.

Responsibilities:
◆ Play the instrument for all regular and special services of the church.
◆ Serve as accompanist for choirs, ensembles and soloists in regular and special rehearsals and performances, as needed.
◆ Play for weddings and funerals as requested.
 • Assist in planning worship services, choir rehearsals and special music events.
◆ Plan and give direction to a training program designed for developing organists/pianists in the church.
◆ Maintain a regular schedule of organ practice and study.
◆ Serve as secretary to the minister of music.
◆ Maintain music ministry files, library and equipment.
◆ Work with the graded choirs as assigned.
◆ Perform other duties as necessary.

─── ⌘⌘⌘◆⌘⌘⌘ ───

Youth Minister

Principal Function: The minister of youth is responsible to the pastor or minister of education for assisting the church in planning, coordinating and promoting the youth programs of the church, special youth projects, assignments and events.

Responsibilities:
- ◆ Work with the ministerial staff, appropriate committees and program leaders in planning, evaluating and coordinating all youth ministries of the church.
- ◆ Conduct special training projects for youth workers.
- ◆ Advise in the use of program materials, equipment, supplies and space by youth groups in all church program organizations.
  - • Plan and direct youth groups in all church program organizations.
- ◆ Plan and direct youth fellowships, retreats and mission trips.
- ◆ Plan and direct parenting seminars and workshops.
- ◆ Counsel youth and parents as needed.
- ◆ Lead in a weekly youth visitation program.
- ◆ Conduct weekly youth Bible study.
- ◆ Develop relationships with local school officials and be available to speak and/or visit in the schools.
- ◆ Remain informed of current trends in youth education programs and youth culture.
- ◆ Be alert to win the lost and assist both workers and youth in reaching the unreached.

* This position is often called minister of students or student minister.

Minister of Recreation (Activities)

Principal Function: The minister of recreation is responsible to the minister of education for planning, conducting and evaluating a program of recreation for church members and other persons in the community.

Responsibilities:
- Direct the planning, coordinating, conducting and evaluating of the recreational activities in the church.
- Coordinate the scheduling and administer the activities in the recreation center.
- Maintain and supervise the repair of recreational facility. Be responsible for the inventory, care, repair and storage of recreation equipment and supplies.
- Work with the nominating committee to recruit and enlist workers for the recreation program.
- Schedule activities of paid and volunteer workers.
- Periodically review and evaluate recreational policies and programs.
- Participate in a weekly hospital and prospect visitation.
- Provide leadership training for both paid and volunteer workers.
- Serve as a recreation resource person and advisor to organizations of the church as requested.
- Provide representation for the church in planning, conducting and evaluating

recreation activities that involve other churches and groups.

◆ Cooperate with associational and state leaders in promoting activities of mutual interest.

Minister of Single Adults (Singles Ministry)

Principal Function: The minister to single adults is responsible to the minister of education for developing, planning, and supervising the total church program for single adults.

Responsibilities:
- Meet regularly with staff members to plan, coordinate and evaluate the single adult ministries.
- Work with appropriate committees, program leaders and ministerial staff to prepare the budget for single adult ministry.
- Plan and conduct effective support ministries (i.e. Bible study, retreats, mission projects and appropriate seminars).
- Counsel single adults as needed.
- Lead single adults to participate in the total church program.
- Work with the nominating committee to enlist and train leaders for single adult ministry.
- Conduct special training projects for single adult workers in proper relationship to the ongoing church program.
- Participate in weekday prospect and hospital visitation.

Minister of Evangelism & Outreach

Principal Function: The minister of evangelism and outreach is responsible to the church. He or she will be supervised by the pastor and will be responsible for the development and promotion of the evangelistic and outreach ministries of the church.

Responsibilities:
◆ Oversee the regular and organized visitation of the church through planning, organizing, and evaluating.
◆ Develop church members to be personal witnesses of their faith in Jesus.
◆ Serve on the Missions Committee of the church as an ex officio member.
◆ Serve on the Sunday School Council and other councils to give input as to evangelism.
◆ Preach in the absence of the pastor or when requested by the church.
◆ Accept pastoral visitation responsibilities as assigned by the pastor.
◆ Serve on the ministerial staff, accepting responsibilities as a member.
◆ Assist the pastor, staff and church in outreach and other community ministries.
◆ Keep informed on evangelistic and witnessing resources, materials, methods, and administration; cooperating with denominational personnel, developments and interests.
◆ Recommend an annual estimated budget for evangelistic and outreach needs.
◆ Perform others duties as assigned by the pastor.

Minister of Adults

Principal Function: The minister of adult work is responsible to the minister of education for assisting church program organizations to develop a comprehensive program of adult education. Consult with other staff members concerning activities, policies and procedures that relate to their areas of responsibility.

Responsibilities:
◆ Work with program organization leaders to enlist adult workers.
◆ Conduct special training projects for adult workers in proper relationship to the church training program.
◆ Advise in the use of program materials, equipment, supplies and space by adult groups in all church program organizations.
◆ Work with other staff members to provide needed services.
◆ Assist with planning and conducting special projects (such as camps and retreats) for adult program organization groups.
◆ Work with organization leaders to coordinate visitation for the adult division and lead workers to visit prospects and absentees.
◆ Work with program leaders, teachers and appropriate staff members to resolve philosophical, procedural and scheduling problems in the adult division.

Minister of Children's Work

Principal Function: The minister of children's work is responsible to the minister of education for overseeing the planning, coordinating and implementing of a program for children from birth through sixth grade.

Responsibilities:
- Work with key leaders in the hiring of paid workers and enlisting of volunteers in the birth through sixth grade programs.
- Conduct special training projects for children's workers in proper relationship to the church program.
- Periodically review church policies and programs with appropriate staff or committees and bring recommendations for needed changes and improvements to the church.
- Assist the staff in planning for and presentation of annual budgets and in overseeing the expenditures of funds.
- Keep abreast of new materials, programs and methods, etc.
- Work with the media services and minister of recreation to provide needed services.
- Assist with planning and conducting special projects, camps, retreats, etc., for children's organizations.
- Organize and oversee an ongoing visitation and evangelism program for children and parents.

- Organize and oversee a new Christian orientation program for middle and older children.
- Cooperate with associational and state leaders in promoting activities of mutual interest.

Media Director

Principal Function: The media director classifies and catalogs all library and media inventory and directs the church media ministry.

Responsibilities
- Supervise and coordinate the activities of the library volunteers.
- Keep an up-to-date library card file.
- Purchase and repair all books and audiovisual aids.
- Assist in the distribution of program organization literature.
- Promote the ministry of church media.

Church Hostess

Principal Function: The church hostess works with the business administrator in overseeing the scheduling, menu selection, purchasing, preparation, and serving including the cleanup involved in food services.

Responsibilities:
- Train and supervise kitchen staff members and volunteer servers.
- Plan menus for weekday ministries, Wednesday night supper and special occasions as requested.
- Purchase all necessary food items.
- Maintain high standards of sanitation in the kitchen area to comply with local health and sanitation laws.
- Maintain an up-to-date inventory of food supplies.
- Arrange for servicing, repairing and replacing equipment in the kitchen as needed.
- Work with the maintenance staff on table and room arrangements for all meals and social functions.
- Maintain accurate records of supplies, costs and operation.

Custodian

Principal Function: The custodian is responsible for maintaining clean buildings and grounds and for making minor equipment repairs.

Responsibilities:
- Maintain floors (sweep, mop, and buff, clean and wax); dust furniture and equipment; wash walls and windows; and, vacuum carpets according to schedule.
- Maintain clean restrooms and replenish supplies.
- Request cleaning and maintenance supplies and equipment as needed.
- Operate heating and cooling equipment according to schedule and instructions.
- Prepare baptistery for use as directed. Clean baptistery and adjoining areas following baptism.
- Open and close the facilities daily as scheduled.
- Maintain yard area and parking lot surrounding church buildings.
- Check with supervisor daily for special assignments.
- Move furniture, set up tables and chairs for suppers, banquets and other similar occasions; set up educational areas for regular and special activities as assigned.
- Prepare facilities for special use as requested by supervisor.
- Make minor repairs as directed.
- Paint facilities and equipment as needed.

- Assist when facilities and arrangements are needed for weddings and funerals.
- Report general repair needs to supervisor.

Ministry Assistant (Secretary)

Principal Function: The secretary (ministry assistant) will perform general office work in relieving the supervisor of certain executive and clerical duties.

Responsibilities:
- Transcribe dictation; type sermons; use word processing equipment as required.
- Perform general office work; maintain supplies and various files; keep records and compile these into periodic or occasional reports.
- Review, open and distribute mail; prepare routine answers without direction for approval and signature; answer routine letters in absence of supervisor.
- Act as required during supervisor's absence in making decisions or taking any necessary action not requiring supervisory approval.
- Receive callers, personal or telephone; keep calendar of appointments.
- Notify committee members of meeting dates.
- Perform other duties as requested.

Note: Some other titles for this position may be receptionist, church clerk, office assistant, executive secretary, personal assistant and many others.

Receptionist

Principal Function: The receptionist is responsible for greeting and providing information to all people entering the church office and directing them to their proper destination.

Responsibilities:

◆ Answer the telephone, transfer calls to proper office and/or take messages.

◆ Maintain church calendar and inform appropriate staff of activities.

◆ Prepare hospital list for staff visitation.

◆ Inform staff of membership needs related to illness and death.

◆ Accept additional responsibilities as assigned.

Note: Some other titles for this position may be secretary, church clerk, office assistant, executive secretary, personal assistant and many others.

Pastor's Ministry Assistant

Principal Function: The pastor's secretary serves as personal secretary to the pastor and performs general duties related to this office.

Responsibilities:
◆ Transcribe and type pastor's correspondence.
◆ Type and file pastor's sermons.
◆ Serve as pastor's receptionist and make appointments for him.
◆ Maintain office files and records.
◆ Notify baptismal candidates and make arrangements for baptismal services.
◆ Prepare Sunday worship service information each week and submit to local news media.
◆ Prepare information for Sunday order of service.
◆ Serve as corresponding secretary for deacons.
◆ Relieve church receptionist as needed.
◆ Accept additional responsibilities as assigned.

Education Ministry Assistant

Principal Function: The education secretary serves as personal ministry assistant to the minister of education and maintains accurate records related to the program organizations of the church.

Responsibilities:
◆ Type general correspondence as needed.
◆ Serve as receptionist and appointment secretary.
◆ Maintain office files and records.
◆ Assist in preparation of special materials for program ministries of the church.
◆ Maintain an up-to-date prospect file.
◆ Place the order for and prepare organization literature for distribution.
◆ Prepare and update the church calendar.

Children Ministry Assistant

Principal Function: The children's work secretary serves as secretary to the director of children's work.

Responsibilities:
- Type all correspondence for children's work programs.
- Maintain office files and records.
- Prepare materials for church programs related to preschoolers and children.
- Maintain personal data and accounts receivable records for preschool and children's kindergarten and day care.
- Assist director in planning work schedules, curriculum and activities for preschool and children's day care.
- Assist children's work director in pupil placement, class organization, faculty meetings and training for staff.
- Maintain records of kindergarten and day care staff personnel.
- Accept additional responsibilities as deemed necessary.

Trustees

Principal Functions: Act as legal agents or representatives as directed by the church, signing all legal documents involving the purchase, sale, mortgaging and rental church property, only upon direction by the church.

Responsibilities:
◆ Maintain inventory of all legal documents, in conjunction with clerk.
◆ Counsel with church staff, key leaders, committees or organizations concerning legal matters.
◆ Hold legal title to all church property (as required by state law) and act only as directed by the church in regular or special business meetings.
◆ Make recommendations to the church concerning legal documents, property and other legal issues.

*Note: If the church is incorporated, Corporate Officers will be elected annually by the church. Their duties will be clarified in the Bylaws, similar to this suggested description of Trustees.

Moderator

Principal Functions: Work with the other key leaders and church staff to develop an agenda for the church business meetings.

Responsibilities:
◆ Maintain the church fellowship through information and participation.
◆ Conduct orderly business meetings following church bylaws and parliamentary procedure, using a fair and impartial manner.
◆ Clarify church business for later action.
◆ Keep the business meetings on course.
◆ Consult with church staff and clerk in preparation of and evaluation of the church business meeting agenda.
◆ Speak for the church in times of crises.
◆ Evaluate the business meetings of the church and propose changes when necessary, in consultation with other key leaders

Financial Ministry Assistant

Principal Function: The financial secretary is responsible for maintaining the church financial records and preparing financial reports.

Responsibilities:
♦ Receive, count and deposit all church offerings.
♦ Post receipts and disbursements of all accounts according to financial system.
♦ Post the weekly offerings to individual accounts.
♦ Reconcile the bank statement monthly.
♦ Prepare monthly and annual financial reports for finance committee, deacons and church business meetings.
♦ Prepare quarterly and annual government reports.
♦ Check and total all invoices when approved; inform the responsible persons of their budget expenditure.
♦ Receive and answer questions about financial matters.
♦ Maintain a file of invoices, correspondence and reports.
♦ Prepare and issue checks to staff members, designations and organizations in accordance with approved church policy.
♦ Mail pledge cards, stewardship letters and envelopes to new members.
♦ Assist in planning and promoting the annual stewardship campaign.
♦ Perform other tasks as requested.

Treasurer (Financial Secretary)

Principal Functions: Maintain adequate records of all church funds received and disbursed, reconciling bank statements and correct ledgers as needed.

Responsibilities:
◆ Record individual contributions to the church and provide quarterly and annual reports.
◆ Sign checks in accordance with church policies and procedures; examining supporting data for all check requests and issue checks for co-signature.
◆ Make monthly and annual financial reports to the appropriate church committees, the deacons, and the church business meetings.
◆ Serve as assigned or be ex officio member of church organizations such as the Budget (Finance) Committee, Personnel Committee, trustees, and/or deacons.
◆ Recommend policies and procedures to the appropriate church committees, bodies, boards, and organizations for receiving, accounting, disbursing, and reporting church monies.
◆ Supervise or assist in the supervision of an accounting system that provides adequate internal controls to protect all funds and workers.
◆ Ensure that funds and gifts are used according to instruction from the

congregation or as directed by the contributor.

◆ Update and maintain guidelines approved by the Internal Revenue Service for the provision of tax credits which involve non-cash gifts.

Chapter 4 Effective Church Committees

As an educator, I have served on numerous committees and attended committee meetings that seemed to go on forever. What makes it so wasteful of time is that I could never see who benefited from the time spent nor did I see any decisions made. I realized I was spending a lot of time in those meetings that could be used for productive teaching. To be sure, not all committees are bad, and not all committee meetings are unnecessary.

Pastors and church leaders must count on their leadership teams. The more you build intentional leadership in your ministry, the better chance of setting your church up for long term success, even after the current leaders have gone off the scene (Price T, n.d.).

When a committee begins to manage details, it becomes overwhelmingly tedious and ineffective. Setting direction will get the most bang for the buck from your leaders and committee members. Whether you are a pastor leading a committee, a chair of a committee or a church committee member, here are some principles that may help you focus, engage as a team and move forward.

Spend More Time On Future Plans Than Present Issues. Committees, as a general rule, should spend more time talking about future plans. Take a look at your next agenda and mark the items that relate to the future direction and vision of the church. If it's too lopsided toward putting out current fires, figure out a way to solve present day issues quickly, then move on to planning, dreaming and strategizing for the future of your church.

Build Meetings Around Big Points, Not Small Ones. As you are creating your agenda, be sure to build the meeting around the big rocks – what are the foundational things that need to be discussed in conversation? Work on those first and foremost.

Craft Your Meeting Agenda Well And In Advance. Don't have a meeting without an agenda. Be sure you know what needs to be covered and use the best practices for circulating the agenda in advance, holding the conversation to the topic at hand, etc.

Delegate Regularly. A committee trying to plan out details together will take forever! It may feel like you are doing something, but in reality, valuable time is being wasted. Committees must delegate management, planning and other tasks to individuals, other leaders or sub-teams.

Refine, Don't Design. Board meetings are not good places to design nitty gritty programming and ministries. There may be a time when some questions need to be asked of those in charge. There may be some needed accountability for an area of ministry or department that is lagging behind. Committees need to step in and help refine things, but don't get involved in daily operations. It will become impossible.

Stay Within Time Parameters. Meetings should start on time and end on time. This is not only a good habit, but it's a gift to give to your people and a great culture of which to be a part.

Schedule Some Of Your Meetings To Focus Heavily On Prayer. You should invest time at each meeting for prayer and you should encourage committee members to pray for their work together and the church. Additionally, some meetings should be set aside to focus solely on prayer. I knew of a church once where all the newly formed committees met in January (or for the first time) and just prayed for the church and the ministries. That was their only agenda item (Price T (n.d.).

Suggestions for Strengthening a Committee

- ◆ Understand your committee's task (secure task description).
- ◆ Understand the relationship of your committee to other committees in the church body.
- ◆ Understand the role of each member of the committee as it relates to the other members.
- ◆ Do a thorough job (quality before quantity).
- ◆ Be creative following the leadership of the Holy Spirit.
- ◆ Enjoy your ministry through the committee's work.
- ◆ Report to the church.

Dos & Don'ts of Committee Meetings

- Be courteous to all members.
- Always deal with the issue or problem at hand.
- Develop a kind, trusting relationship with other members of the committee.
- Be fair to everyone, even those who disagree with you.
- Never lose your cool in a committee meeting.
- Don't let anyone press your panic button.
- Avoid putting other persons down.
- Don't get involved in personalities, keep the discussion on issues.
- When you feel compelled to disagree, do it in a diplomatic way.
- Learn to be completely honest and open.
- Remember that most people do not make decisions logically but emotionally.
- Never attempt to force your conclusions on other members.
- Plan and distribute an agenda in advance.
- Start and stop on time.

Reasons for Committee Meetings

◆ Information giving and receiving
◆ Planning
◆ Problem-solving
◆ Decision making
◆ Social and inspirational
◆ Therapeutic - Response to someone who has been hurt

Chapter 5 Job Descriptions for Committees

Within the church we will find groups of people who meet together to brainstorm, strategize, make recommendations or decisions and plans on how to effectively do ministry in a certain area of church life.

◆ Church Board (called by varying names in different churches but composed of those who provide broad oversight of the church)
◆ Long Standing Committees or Ministry Teams(composed of leaders of a department or ministry area, i.e., Christian Education Commission)
◆ Short Term or Temporary Committees or Ministry Teams (composed of select individuals to work on strategic planning for a seasonal ministry i.e., VBS, task i.e., Budget Committee, or what we might call a steering committee to help with new ministry initiatives)

While these groups may have different functions, the church's purpose should provide the common thread:

◆ The Church's Purpose determines their reason for existence.
◆ You should be able to provide a rational for why this group is needed to help the church fulfill its purpose. If not, it is possibly wasting precious time and resources.
◆ The Church's Purpose is the end toward which all work.

- The church purpose should be used as a grid through which all decisions are made. If not, it is possibly fragmenting rather than unifying the church.

The Church Purpose is what helps all the various ministries remain coordinated within the church. No committee, board, department, or team should be an end to itself. Yet, within the framework of the church's purpose, great freedom can be given.

Activities & Recreation Committee

Principal Functions: Develop a program of activities and recreation for the total church family and those to whom the church should minister.

Responsibilities:
◆ Develop policies for the use of activity and recreational facilities and equipment.
◆ Promote church-wide activities and recreational opportunities.
◆ Make recommendations for securing and maintaining equipment.
◆ Work with the Building and Grounds Committee in the maintenance of church activity and recreational facilities.
◆ Make recommendations to the Budget (Finance) Committee on budget needs for this ministry.
◆ Serve as a resource team for the church family and the respective ministerial staff committee when calling a minister of activities and recreation.

Audio Services (Sound) Committee

Principal Functions: Research and recommend the audio needs for the worship center and other facilities.

Responsibilities:
◆ Enlist and train sound operators for worship services and special events.
◆ Provide a maintenance program for upkeep of the equipment.
◆ Evaluate constantly the audio ministry of church and recommend changes in the audio system.
◆ Make recommendations to the Budget (Finance) Committee for maintenance of and new equipment needs.

Audit Committee

Principal Functions: Conduct an annual review of the church financial records and make a report to the church. The frequency of the audit(s) will be determined by church financial policies.

Responsibilities:
◆ Secure an independent audit of the church financial records and system when requested, or according to church policy, and make the report to the church.
◆ Make recommendations concerning church financial records, accounting system, personnel, equipment and operations to the church and respective church leaders.
◆ Clarify to the church the types of audits available and needed by the church at various times and situations.
◆ Assist the treasurer, financial ministry assistant, budget (Finance) Committee, pastor, staff and deacons on financial operations, policies, effectiveness, efficiency, tax reporting, federal and state laws compliance and other financial matters as requested.

Baptism Committee

Principal Functions: Make sure that all necessary baptismal equipment and facilities are available and ready prior to each baptismal service.

Responsibilities:
- Notify candidates for baptism well in advance of the scheduled baptism, and provide the pastor with a list of those to be present.
- Arrange with the pastor and candidates for a period of instruction regarding the baptism.
- Prepare name tags of candidates for identification purposes.
- Keep an official record of baptisms.
- Assist candidates during the baptism.
- Assist the pastor at baptismal time.
- Perform necessary cleanup after the baptism.
- Conduct annual inspections of the baptismal facilities and equipment.
- Recommend to the Building and Grounds Committee additional or different equipment and space as needed.
- Serve as a resource in the church about the ordinance of baptism.

Benevolence Committee

Principal Functions: Develop, recommend and oversee policies and procedures which establish the type, amount, and frequency of assistance to individuals or families who request assistance.

Responsibilities:
- Locate church members and community persons who can provide appropriate assistance.
- Work with other groups in the church which provide benevolent actions and make recommendations of these ministries.
- Survey and determine available community agencies and their resources.
- Make recommendation to Budget (Finance) Committee for monies needed for ministering to people and coordinate special funding provisions for benevolent ministries.
- Investigate and administer benevolence resources as needed.
- Make reports to the church according to policy.
- Inform and involve the church members to support benevolent ministry.

Budget (Finance) Committee

Principal Functions: Coordinate the submission of program financial needs and prepare an annual itemized budget for approval by the church,

Responsibilities:
◆ Recommend and maintain appropriate fiscal policies for the church.
◆ Prepare with the treasurer and/or financial secretary a monthly financial report of all receipts and disbursements for the business meeting.
◆ Coordinate fiscal and personnel activities with church staff, committees, and programs.
◆ Provide an annual report of all financial activities (receipts, disbursements and investments) to the church.
◆ Assist the Audit Committee as requested.
◆ Provide input on non-budgeted items, advice on budget revisions or adjustments, consider special offerings, and make recommendations to the church.
◆ Advise the church on financial transactions as to soundness and effect on the financial structure and standing of the church.
◆ Work closely with the Properties and Insurance Committee and other committees involving church funds as requested.

Note: For more effectiveness, some churches combine this committee with the Stewardship Committee.

Building & Grounds Committee

Principal Functions: Oversee the safekeeping, protection, maintenance and repair of church facilities, furnishing, and attached equipment such as heating, cooling, lighting and storage.

Responsibilities:
◆ Make sure that all furnishings and equipment are properly working.
◆ Make recommendations on replacement of worn items or equipment, landscaping, and care of grounds and parking facilities.
◆ Make recommendations to the Budget (Finance) Committee as to necessary funds to provide for the annual maintenance of all facilities, furnishings and grounds.
◆ Take actions in emergency situations regarding church facilities, furnishings and grounds.
◆ Serve as a resource team when the church considers securing additional or selling property and furnishings.
◆ Serve as a resource team in facility safety, security and crime prevention issues.
◆ Conduct annual inventory, inspection and evaluation of all church property and equipment.
◆ Make recommendations concerning maintenance and usage of church parking facilities and signage.
◆ Assist and support the church custodial personnel in matters related to the building and grounds.

* *Note: This committee often is called maintenance, property & Space, facilities management, or house & grounds.*

Building Steering Committee

Principal Functions: The building steering committee is the group of church members who act on behalf of the church leadership and congregation to guide the project through the programming, budgeting, design and construction process. The steering committee oversees and directs the work of the church building team

Responsibilities: during three phases

Survey Phase
◆ Obtain training and assistance from state and national agencies.
◆ Evaluate the existing church property and buildings.
◆ Involve the church to answers: What facilities are needed? What can and should be done to existing facilities? Is additional property needed?
◆ Explore community needs to discover opportunities.
◆ Begin preliminary financial understanding and planning.
◆ Present to the church a detailed report of facility and furnishing needs and long-range plans to meet needs.

Planning Phase
◆ Develop a comprehensive building program statement.
◆ Obtain professional assistance from architectural or design firms.

- Present a detailed report of plans, finances and phases of work to be done by the church.
- Work with the architect as preliminary and design drawings are developed.

Construction Phase

- Secure construction drawings and order furnishings.
- Secure bids and award the contract for construction.
- Monitor construction and prepare to occupy the building.
- Makes plans for Dedication Day, transition of facilities, etc.

Cemetery Committee

Principal Functions: Make recommendations to the church concerning issues and policies involving the cemetery.

Responsibilities:
- ◆ Make recommendations to the church concerning cemetery personnel, maintenance, landscaping and any renovations.
- ◆ Keep accurate records of cemetery plots, containing interments as well as those reserved by individuals and families.
- ◆ Serve as resource team in the event of cemetery expansion and the safe-guarding of historical cemetery records.
- ◆ Make recommendations concerning cemetery financial matters.

Committee on Committee

Principal Functions: Select, enlist, and nominate persons to serve on the church committees for church approval.

Responsibilities:
◆ Survey the congregation about spiritual gifts and interests.
◆ Select committee members to ensure a balance of representation.
◆ Assist the pastor, staff and other key leaders with the church's ministry through the committees.
◆ Review annually the number and kinds of committees and the ministry description of each committee and recommend change involving structure, membership, election, addition or deletion.
◆ Review church policies and procedures concerning committees.
◆ Plan training events for committee chairpersons and members.
◆ Serve as a resource team for and make recommendations concerning special (ad hoc or temporary) committees.

Constitution Bylaws Policies Committee

Principal Functions: Determine rules of administration and fundamental matters, such as church doctrine and the disposition of property.

Responsibilities:
◆ Determine the content for the Constitution and Bylaws.[13] *See footnote for an example*
◆ Locate and compile all written copies of Policies and Procedures the church has already approved.
◆ Interview all program leaders, council chairpersons, committee chairpersons and staff to discover what policies and procedures are being used that have not been written down.
◆ Codify all policies and procedures that are being used, but have not been written down as discovered by the interviews conducted in Step 3.
◆ Compile and assimilate a comprehensive first-draft document or committee consideration of a proposed Constitution and Bylaws.
◆ Agree on a comprehensive first-draft document.
◆ Take the comprehensive first-draft document, section by section, back to the program groups, councils, committees, and

---

13
http://storage.cloversites.com/arkansasbaptiststateconventi on/documents/constitution%202.pdf

111

staff affected by the documents to obtain additional input.

♦ Make necessary changes to each section of the document after completing step 7 and agree on them in committee.

♦ Bring each section of the completed document to the church for approval and implementation.

♦ Receive suggestions, input, matters referred from the church, etc., and make recommendations back to the church on these issues and other matters concerning Constitution-Bylaws and Policies.

Flower & Decorations Committee

Principal Functions: Recommend policies and procedures for acquiring, arranging, and disposing of flowers and decorations for worship services and special events.

Responsibilities:
- ◆ Recommend policies related to providing flowers for sick and bereaved members and special occasions for the church.
- ◆ Work with the Stewardship (or Budget) Committee in requesting the flower and decorations committee financial support in the annual budget.
- ◆ Acquire, place, and dispose of flower arrangements and special decorations.
- ◆ Serve as a resource team in planning, designing and renovation of existing or new worship and storage space.

Food Service Committee

Principal Functions: Consult with church leaders to determine the food service needs of the church. Develop and recommend policies and procedures related to food service for kitchen operation, meal scheduling, and facilities use.

Responsibilities:
◆ Recommend food service to be provided.
◆ Communicate approved food service policies and procedures to the church.
◆ Recommend to the Personnel Committee the needed personnel for the food service program.
◆ Recommend to the Budget (Finance) Committee the money needed for food service. • Coordinate the total food service operation of the church.
◆ Evaluate food service and report to the church as needed.
◆ Assist the food service director.
◆ Assist in planning for an efficient system for making reservations and collecting money for meals.

History & Heritage Committee

Principal Functions: Locate and preserve all the historical records and other related materials of the church. Assist the church in making and keeping accurate, comprehensive records of its current life and work.

Responsibilities:
◆ Develop and recommend policies and procedures to the church regarding its historical documents and materials.
◆ Communicate the heritage of the church and of the larger heritage as Baptists at large to the church.
◆ Assist the church with special occasions such as Homecoming, Memorial Sundays, Centennial Celebration, or Heritage Days.
◆ Undergird and strengthen the life and ministry of the church by providing support for the past, present and future.
◆ Serve as a resource team for the church in the design, construction or renovation of a History and Heritage Room in the church facility.

Strategic Planning Committee
(long-range)

Principal Functions: Enlist training assistance and resources from the state convention office and other sources outside the church to elect officers and specify duties of committee members to lead the church to adopt mission, vision and core value statements.

Responsibilities:
◆ Engage the church through various activities to assist in answering the question, "What is God's will for us and what the needs in our church and community are?"
◆ Set goals for the church, which if accomplished, will meet needs.
◆ Plan strategies for reaching the goals.
◆ Compile and present a comprehensive report to the church.
◆ Establish an evaluation and implementation process for the long-range activities.
◆ Make periodic reports to the church on the progress of the plans.

Lord's Supper Committee

Principal Functions: Assist the pastor and deacons in planning the schedule for the observance of the Lord's Supper.

Responsibilities:
◆ Maintain an inventory of all Lord's Supper equipment and request additional equipment as needed.
◆ Maintain an adequate supply of materials used for the Lord's Supper and purchase additional supplies as needed.
◆ See that all necessary Lord's Supper equipment and supplies are in place prior to each observance of the Lord's Supper.
◆ Arrange for all Lord's Supper equipment to be gathered, cleaned, and properly stored after each observance.
◆ Clean and put back in order the area used in preparing for the Lord's Supper.
◆ Evaluate the work of the committee by receiving feedback from the pastor, deacons, and church regarding ways to improve planning and preparation.

Media Library Committee

Principal Functions: Maintain an adequate library of church media, books, materials, periodicals and equipment.

Responsibilities:
- ◆ Promote the use of media-library services and materials available to the church membership and programs.
- ◆ Work with the Media-Library director in the enlistment and training of volunteer personnel to staff the ministry.
- ◆ Recommend to the Budget (Finance) Committee money needed to support the media-library ministry of the church.
- ◆ Maintain proper organization of the media-library through equipment, schedule of library hours, and resources.
- ◆ Recommend to the church all needed media-library materials, services and equipment.

Ministerial Staff Position Search Committee

Principal Functions: Determine the criteria for this staff position and other guide lines for accomplishing the committee's purpose such as salary, benefits, ministry position description, church information, input of pastor and other staff members as well as church personnel policy. [A local church's Bylaws may specify how the church proceeds with the election and formulation of the needed staff position committee and how the respective committee conducts its work.]

Responsibilities:
- Organize the committee by election of officers and clarification of committee members' duties and responsibilities.
- Secure training and resources from the associational and state convention offices.
- Receive and evaluate resumes and process other information.
- Study the information on a short list of potential prospects.
- Focus on one candidate at a time, investigate thoroughly this person and make decisions on this minister.
- Present this candidate to the church with thorough information and opportunity to meet with the candidate, spouse and family.
- Extend a call to the candidate, assuming a favorable vote of the church, and relay his/her answer to the church.
- Assist in moving the candidate to the church, helping in the transition to the new community, and supporting this new staff

person in beginning their ministry at the church.

◆ Serve as this new staff person's ministerial relations committee ("support group") in the transition time (up to six months or a year).

Ministry Credentials Committee

Principal Functions: [This committee shall be considered a standing or permanent committee. The membership of and the election of the committee's chairperson shall be according to the church's policies on committees.] Shall be comprised of five (5) persons nominated to the church by the Nominating Committee. Shall serve the church to investigate a member's call to the ministry.

Responsibilities:
♦ Shall recommend to the church for licensing to the gospel ministry.
♦ Shall also serve the church as the group which arranges investigation and response to a member's request or another church's request for ordination of the member to the gospel ministry.
♦ Shall recommend that the church proceed with the ordination service (if the committee has served as the ordination council).
♦ Shall also serve with the pastor and staff to teach, emphasize and resource the membership on the biblical, historical and practical aspects of ordination

Missions Development Committee

Principal Functions: Promote missions (local, associational, state, North American and international) in the church through prayer support, activities, publicity, information and the seasonal special offerings.

Responsibilities:
- ◆ Plan special worship services or emphases on missions in consultation with the pastor, staff and mission program leaders such as the Women's Ministry (Woman's Missionary Union director), Men's Ministry leader (Brotherhood director) and other missions leaders in the church.
- ◆ Recommend mission trips and necessary support to the church.
- ◆ Serve as resource team for or liaison between the church and operating missions of the church.
- ◆ Study the new mission possibilities and make recommendations to the church about such new starts.
- ◆ Make recommendations to the Budget (Finance) Committee as to the needed money for missions support for the annual church budget.
- ◆ Recommend mission involvement and leadership policies and guidelines to the church.

Music Committee

Principal Functions: Serve as the Minister of Music Search Committee and the Personnel Committee for the accompanists and any related persons hired or selected by the church in the ministry of music (unless stated otherwise by the Bylaws). Their actions shall constitute a recommendation to the church family.

Responsibilities:

◆ Be comprised of the following persons (unless otherwise determined by the Bylaws): the minister of music (ex-officio member), the accompanists and their associates, leaders of youth-children-preschool music and three other church members

◆ Assist the minister of music in planning the annual calendar for the music and worship ministry in the church.

◆ Elect committee officers. Composition of and officers for this committee may be determined by the church Bylaws.

◆ Assist him/her in the planning and conducting of fellowship and spiritual growth events for choir-music support persons.

◆ Assist the minister of music to organize music for special events and ministries of the church (i.e., Homecoming, revival, holidays, etc.).

◆ Receive suggestions, analyze data and make recommendations to the church concerning instruments, audio systems, and related items.

- Serve as the Minister of Music Search Committee and the Personnel Committee for the accompanists and any related persons hired or selected by the church in the ministry of music (unless stated otherwise by the Bylaws). Their actions shall constitute a recommendation to the church family.
- Recommend a budget for the music ministry (but not salary and benefits) to the Budget (Finance) Committee for the annual budget.
- Serve as a resource team on matters deemed important to the music and worship ministry of the church.

New Member Assimilation Committee

Principal Functions: Greet visitors each Sunday, hold classes as well as membership ceremonies at least twice a year, help visitors and members find places to connect within the congregation, provide appropriate publications relating to membership, maintain contact with friends and members who come irregularly, provide caring for those in need.

Responsibilities

◆ Assist the pastor and staff members in the assimilation of new members into the fellowship and ministry of the church.

◆ Recommend activities, programs and necessary financial support for new member assimilation.

◆ Work with the minister of education (and/or Christian Development or Discipleship), Discipleship Training and Family Ministry directors of the church for classes, seminars, study opportunities, mentoring and discipleship needs for new members.

◆ Plan and conduct new member fellowships.

◆ Assist the pastor and staff members in the planning and conducting of new member classes which may be mandatory for membership.

◆ Plan and promote new membership opportunities and emphases with the deacon ministry.

Nominating Committee

Principal Functions: Select, interview, and enlist church program organizational leaders, church emphasis program leaders, general officers and certain committees (if designated by church Bylaws), before they are presented to the church for church approval.

Responsibilities:
◆ Screen and approve volunteers before they are invited to serve.
◆ Distribute the most capable leadership among the most pressing needs of the church.
◆ Assist in discovering and enlisting persons to fill leadership and abilities of church members.
◆ Devise methods of discovering potential leaders and the gifts and abilities of church members.
◆ Present the names of volunteers to be elected by the church.
◆ Coordinate the filling of vacancies of volunteer workers and leaders as they occur during the church year.

Note: This committee is sometimes called ministry placement Committee

Pastor Search Committee

Principal Functions: Determine the criteria for recommending a pastor and other guidelines for accomplishing the committee's purpose.

Responsibilities:
- Secure training and resources from the state convention office or other outside source.
- Conduct an evaluation of the church involving its members.
- Evaluate the candidates from resumes and other processed information, using the utmost care and confidentiality.
- Select promising candidates from personal contact and deal with one candidate at a time from the committee's short list.
- Recommend the best candidate to the church after much prayer, contacts and information; using a thorough presentation time and information process with the church.
- Facilitate the relocation of the new pastor and his family to the church and community.
- Follow through in helping the new pastor make a smooth transition into the church and community.
- Plan a Pastor Installation Service and other appropriate related events which help the pastor and family in this new location.

Personnel Committee

Principal Functions: Assist the staff and other key leaders concerning the need for additional church staff positions and when there are staff vacancies.

Responsibilities:
◆ Prepare and update, as necessary, ministry position descriptions for all employed personnel.
◆ Prepare and maintain an organizational manual relating to the church's employed personnel.
◆ Recruit, interview, and recommend to the church new employees.
◆ Develop and recommend salaries and benefits for employees in all classifications.
◆ Develop and recommend policies and procedures to the church for employed personnel administration.
◆ Consult annually with the Budget (Finance) Committee in budgeting for current and future employee salary schedule and benefit provisions.
◆ Assess ministry (job) performance of each staff member at least annually and be sensitive to job insecurities that may plague them.

Preschool Committee

Principal Functions: Recommend and publicize preschool policies and procedures related to the church's ministry to children from birth until entry into the first grade.

Responsibilities:
◆ Recommend the purchase of furnishings, equipment and supplies for preschool ministry.
◆ Coordinate along with the church staff space assigned to various preschool ministries. In churches with weekday education ministries this action requires coordination with the Church Weekday Education Committee and the Weekday Director.
◆ Work with the personnel committee and/or the pastor to select, train and supervise employed preschool teachers.
◆ Communicate regularly with the pastor, church staff and the Church Leadership Team.
◆ Help publicize preschool ministries to the church and community.

Property & Space Committee

Principal Functions: Inspect properties and maintain inventory of equipment and furnishings.

Responsibilities:
◆ Conduct annual evaluation of space allocations to determine better uses of property, space and furnishings.
◆ Recommend space rearrangements for best usage of facilities.
◆ Recommend acquisition and maintenance of mission property.
◆ Recommend training and supervision of maintenance personnel.
◆ Develop and recommend maintenance policies and procedures.
◆ Recommend policies regarding space, properties, and equipment.
◆ Develop and recommend insurance plan for buildings and properties.
◆ Prepare budget and administer the maintenance budget.
◆ Oversee bus and van needs, if such a committee does not exist.
◆ Determine needs of, arrange, equip, and administer parking space.
◆ Select and maintain adequate furnishings for programs and activities.
◆ Assist church committees in responsibilities relating to property.
◆ Promote conservation of energy and other natural resources.
◆ Recommend survey, planning, and building committee when needed.

- Evaluate property and buildings to ensure that space is accessible to disabled persons and the elderly.
- Evaluate building and grounds security and make recommendations.
- Evaluate the need for signs and maintain existing signs.
- Recognize and train other members interested in joining this committee.

Public Relations Committee

Principal Functions: Determine within the church and community the understanding and acceptance of the church's work.

Responsibilities:
◆ Develop with organizational leaders a plan to interpret the church's work to the public.
◆ Use appropriate media to communicate the church's work to the general public and community.
◆ Increase members' awareness of the values of good church public relations and media support.
◆ Recommend policies, procedures, and actions to improve church public relations and media ministry.

Stewardship Committee

Principal Functions: Review the committee's purpose, areas of concern, and basic responsibilities in the matters of careful and responsible management of the church organization, including its mission, goals, and values.

Responsibilities:
◆ Study what the Bible teaches about stewardship including giving.
◆ Study, identify, and write out the mission of the church.
◆ Seek to understand the church's stewardship needs.
◆ Work with Budget (Finance) Committee on proposed annual budget.
◆ Plan and calendar the emphases and opportunities that will best help the church promote the annual church budget and faithful giving.
◆ Seek the cooperation of other church leaders and use all existing channels of the church to communicate biblical stewardship truths, with emphasis on personal stewardship and spiritual growth.
◆ Become familiar with and determine the best available methods and resources for implementing planned stewardship activities.
◆ Be sensitive to stewardship needs that are unique or that do not occur regularly.

Ushers Committee

Principal Functions: Enlist and recommend ushers and greeters to serve at all services, arriving early for worship services (30 minutes prior is usual).

Responsibilities:
- Make sure that all appropriate doors are opened and lights are on.
- Check the restrooms and entrance ways for cleanliness.
- Check thermostat settings for appropriate cooling and heating.
- Pick up any trash on church pews, straighten hymnal rack materials and make sure worship center furnishings are in place.
- Make sure worship guides (bulletins), offering plates, guest cards, and other needed materials are ready and available.
- Be clear on the order of worship. Introduce guests to pastor, staff and members.
- Greet people with a smile, a warm word of welcome, an introduction of yourself and provide them with a worship guide.
- Assist people with information, materials, and seating as needed.
- Assist people as needed after the conclusion of the service.
- Assist in the formal welcome of guests and any special guests.
- Assist in gathering, counting, and depositing of the offering as per church financial policy.
- Make recommendations concerning safety and crime prevention.

- Assist in emergency situations and crises.
- Patrol the church parking lots and facilities as per church policy.

Weekday Education Committee

Principal Functions: Determine policies and procedures for operating and administering the program.

Responsibilities:
◆ Work in coordination with the personnel committee to staff the weekday education program.
◆ Assist the program director in developing a workable budget.
◆ See that the weekday education program and facilities comply with legal and licensing requirements.
◆ Direct public relations efforts to inform, involve, and educate church members and the community about the program.
◆ Coordinate the work of the program with other church activities involving young children.
◆ Review reports and records to ensure proper operation of the program.
◆ Report regularly to the church about the work of the weekday education program.
◆ Organize the involvement of church members and parents as volunteers in the program.

Worship Committee

Principal Functions: Identify the worship needs and opportunities of the congregation.

Responsibilities:
- Study the biblical and historical aspects of worship with the pastor, staff, and music leaders to be able to effectively facilitate worship.
- Evaluate the effectiveness of the church's worship services and serve as a workgroup to offer suggestions for enriching worship.
- Study the needs of the worship center (sanctuary or auditorium) and make recommendations to the church in these areas.
- Assist the pastor and music staff to lead the church in information about, readiness for, and responses to change concerning worship.
- Provide practical worship ideas for special occasions of worship.
- Identify resource persons who can participate in worship leadership.
- Assist when requested to construct weekly orders of worship.
- Assist and support missions, age group, church programs and other ministries leaders in planning special worship services in their respective areas of work.

For ALL the Days of Your Life

Dedicate Time to the Word of God. Set aside a specific amount of time to study the word of God every day. Keep a praise in your mouth and meditate on him during your daily activities. Stay amazed at the "little things".

Resources

Christian Ministry resources (Richard Hammar) Church Administration Handbook (revised) by Bruce P. Powers, editor (Broadman & Holman, 1997)

Church Leadership team Handbook (Sunday school Board of SBC, 1995)

Outside of the United Kingdom, the KJV is in the public domain. Within the United Kingdom, the rights to the KJV are vested in the Crown

Pastor and Staff Search Committee Guide by Don R. Mathis (Life Way Christian Resources, 1998)

Pastor and Staff Recognition Booklet (Pastor/Leadership Development Department, Mississippi Baptist Convention Board)

Mississippi Baptist Convention Board "A Ministry of the Cooperative Program" Pastor/ Leadership Development Department 1.800.748.1651 e-mail:mcdonnell@mbcb.org awoodward@mbcb.org kgordon@mbcb.org

Price, T. (n.d.). Ten Principles for Effective Church Committees. Retrieved January 17, 2019, from http://www.timpriceblog.com/ten-principles-for-effective-church-committees/

Scripture notation marked NIV are taken from the Holy Bible New International Version© NIV® Copyright © 1973, 1978, 1984, International Bible Society.

Support Your Local Pastor, Practical Ways to Encourage Your Minister by Wes Roberts, (Navpress, 1995)

The Authorized Version or King James Version (KJV), 1611, 1769. All scripture quotations are taken from the Kings James Version unless otherwise noted

Torain, J. S. (2014). *Quick guide to personal qualities of the evangelist* (Vol. 1). Raleigh, NC: LULU COM.

The team Builder by Frank r. Lewis (Life Way Christian resources, 1997)

Has This Book Impacted Your Walk with God?

If you now have a better understanding of church organization or want to share your testimony:

Send your email to mstoe29@msn.com or n_torain@hotmail.com.

Like us on Facebook
www.facebook.com/janie.sheeleytorain

About the Author

Janie S. Torain is a retired high school teacher, online assessor and math rater. She has returned to work as an Academic Success Center Assistant at the community college where she earned her first associate degrees in Accounting and Business Administration. She believes that God and education is the key to raise one out of poverty to live and have life more abundantly!

The success of being a first-generation high school and community college graduate, stirred up the fire for lifelong learning. She has a bachelor's degree in Comprehensive Business Education, a master's degree in Education Technology, an educational specialist degree in Curriculum and Instruction, and a doctorate degree in Educational Leadership. . She is also a National Board-certified teacher in Career and Technical Education. She serves her local church and community as an usher, choir member, Sunday school teacher and Evangelist.

She has previously published her dissertation research, *Virtual Learning: Is It Conducive to Student Achievement*, and her master thesis, *An Assessment of the Impact of Technology on the Performance of Exceptional Children in Computer Adaptive Testing in Person County*. She has also written several books: *If I Could Quit School for a Day, A Quick Guide to the Personal*

Qualities of an Evangelist, Character Expectations of Deacons[14], and Power 365[15]

She and her husband, Nathaniel, had 7 children, 26 grandchildren and 6 great grandchildren and live in a small town in North Carolina. She continues to seek God for guidance on how to go in and out among his people. God has given her a special love for teenagers and young adults.

God is a Keeper--On November 15, 2013, the sudden death of the youngest daughter, at the age of 33, left her and her spouse to raise two of her grandchildren a 10-year old boy and an 8-year old girl. They are now teenagers. Life is good!

The Favor of God--In 2008, she was ordained an evangelist at her church where she faithfully serve as Sunday school teacher, choir member, usher, and preach second Sundays. She and her husband spend any "free time" advising the 6 children on how to raise the 25 grandchildren and 5 great grandchildren and **traveling.**

LIFE IS GOOD!

~Joshua 24:15~

[14] http://www.lulu.com/spotlight/torainj

[15]

https://www.iuniverse.com/Bookstore/BookSearchResults.aspx?Search=power%20365

144

Endnotes

[i] Warren, R. (2016, August 10). Organize Your Church on Purpose, Around Giftedness. Retrieved January 2, 2019, from https://pastors.com/organize-your-church-on-purpose-and-giftedness/

[ii] Source of image http://www.srocps.org/site/articles/timeline_of_church_history